AN
INTRODUCTORY
THEOLOGICAL
WORDBOOK

AN
INTRODUCTORY
THEOLOGICAL
WORDBOOK

by
Iris V. and Kendig Brubaker Cully

Philadelphia
THE WESTMINSTER PRESS

LIBRARY OF CONGRESS CATALOG CARD No. 64–10033

PUBLISHED BY THE WESTMINSTER PRESS®
PHILADELPHIA, PENNSYLVANIA 19107
PRINTED IN THE UNITED STATES OF AMERICA

To young people whose growth into adult-
hood we have gladly shared for a little while
within the Christian community at Belcher-
town, Melrose, Haverhill, Evanston

Preface

In order to find one's way around in any field of study, it is necessary to have a speaking acquaintance with the vocabulary involved. This is as true in regard to the Christian religion as in regard to anything else. Theology seeks to set forth understandings about God. The vocabulary of theology has grown out of the life of the church, the study of the Bible, and the total religious experience of Christian people.

Obviously there are too many words related to theology for all of them to be discussed in this theological wordbook. For example, many names of places and persons, as well as many events referred to in the Bible, are omitted. Several excellent Bible concordances, dictionaries, and atlases are available for persons who seek that kind of information. Here we have selected what seem to be the most essential words of a more strictly theological kind.

The reader will remember that large books could be written (and have been) on every single word included. It has been our aim to state only some of the more important matters about each word. Sometimes the words themselves are difficult. The explanations will have to stretch one's thinking too. The fact is, though, that getting better acquainted with the words can help one move into the reality that lies behind the words. Theology is not the reality. Theology is the effort Christians make to explain and interpret the meaning of the reality. The reality itself will grow clearer for those who know what the church and the Bible are referring to in the vocabulary of faith.

Maybe this would be a good word to look up first, unless something else has captured your interest already: *Faith.*

I. V. C.
K. B. C.

Evanston, Illinois

A

ADOPTION   "To adopt" means to make one's own that which does not belong to oneself, but which can benefit by this new relationship. The word is used in many ways. One speaks of "adopting" the habit of getting to school on time. The habit may not come naturally, but it is good. A child may ask to "adopt" a kitten that turns up at the door. The kitten seems to have no home, but now it will have a home with him. When the natural parents cannot provide the kind of home that babies need, they may be adopted by other families. These are special families because the children have been chosen.

The Bible speaks of people being children of God by adoption. To be sure, God is the creator of the whole world and all living creatures. But to be God's child by adoption is a new and special relationship. This means that one has been chosen by God; indeed, that even before the creation of the world he intended this specific form of relationship. Those who have been led to God through his Son, Jesus Christ, know that they are brought into this relationship through Baptism. They are made children of God in a special way. They are adopted as sons in Christ. (See BAPTISM.)

These adopted children have a new status by participating now in the Sonship of Christ. Jesus said: "Who are my mother and my brothers? . . . Whoever does the will of God is my brother, and sister, and mother." (Mark 3:33, 35.) The "will" or intention of God was that those who had been called by Christ should respond to that call and follow him. The new status confers upon the chosen children special privileges. They receive the gift of the Holy Spirit, strengthening them to serve and follow Christ. They receive the right to call God their Father.

So when Christians pray together in the words of the Lord's Prayer, "Our Father who art in heaven," they do not call God "Father" because he created them. They call him thus because Jesus Christ has made them his brothers and they have accepted their responsibilities as sons of God, their Heavenly Father.

ADVENT The word "Advent" is derived from the Latin and means "coming toward." It is a "coming toward" Christmas. It is the season of the church year that begins four Sundays before Christmas as a time of preparation for that holy day.

The preparation for Christmas is made with joy. But Christmas is also solemn and world-shaking. It announces the entrance of God into the midst of his people in the form of the man Jesus. This adds solemnity to joy. One asks, "How shall we prepare to receive the holy One who comes in love to save us?" There is the immediate realization that no one is worthy of this great event, and that only God can make one worthy. The Christian, alone and through the worship of the whole church, looks at himself in the light of God's goodness, seeking forgiveness of his sins and being renewed in faithfulness to his Lord.

In the traditional Christian calendar of Scripture lessons the emphasis on each of the four Sundays in Advent is a reminder of the ways in which the Lord comes. On the first Sunday the story of Jesus' entry into Jerusalem on Palm Sunday is read, reminding the listeners that Jesus came to earth that he might die and rise again. On the second Sunday the Bible itself is highlighted as the word through which the coming of Christ is made known. The third Sunday tells of John the Baptist, who announced the coming of Christ to the people. The fourth Sunday reminds us that Christ will come again in glory and judgment. (Matt. 21:1–

13; Rom. 15:4–13; Luke 21:25–33; Matt. 11:2–10; John 1:19–28.) The Advent hymns echo these themes.

Since the coming of Jesus marks a new beginning in human life, it was logical to make the Advent season the beginning of the church year. There is one beginning for the calendar year (January 1) and one beginning for the school year (September, or some other date). There is also a beginning for each new year in the life of the Christian church: the first Sunday in Advent.

See CHRISTMAS; EPIPHANY.

ALTAR   An altar has been a central focus for actions of worship in many religions and for thousands of years. In its simplest form it was a large rock on which animals were slain as sacrifices. (See SACRIFICE.) The altar was usually associated with holy places. When a holy place was built to indicate the presence of God (the Tabernacle, Solomon's Temple), the altar was placed outside.

The shape that the altar took in Christian churches was that of an oblong table. The offerings placed upon it were the gifts of food and money that the worshipers brought to be used for the needs of the church and as an expression of their devotion. (See OFFERING.)

The earlier blood offerings were no longer used. Christ had given himself freely as sacrifice for sin, and those who turned to him knew what it was to be forgiven. The cross above the altar is a constant reminder of that sacrifice which restores sinful persons into a right relationship with the Holy God. The church remembers that sin is costly and that forgiveness is not an easy thing. Some liturgies for the Lord's Supper are interpreted as a re-presentation of Christ's sacrifice.

The altar is that place in a church building where offerings are laid and upon which the Lord's Supper is celebrated. It may be fixed against the wall at one end of a chancel or it may be moved out, like a table, so that the clergyman and those who assist him in the service may stand back of it, facing the people. Some new churches place a table altar near the very center of the church, and the people surround it. Thus they are reminded that they are gathered together by God in Christ as they remember his death and resurrection and know his living presence in the midst of their common life.

ANGEL   The word "angel" comes from Greek and Hebrew words that mean "messenger." An angel was no ordinary messenger, but the bearer of a message from God. The Bible speaks of "entertaining angels unawares" (Heb. 13:2). This was a possibility because God's messenger might appear in human form, and only those who were faithful servants of God would recognize the message or the messenger.

In earlier stories the term "the angel of the Lord" refers to the belief that God himself appeared in human form (for example, Ex. 3:1–6, where God appears to Moses from the burning bush). Later Old Testament writings avoid this phrase.

Again, angels are supernatural beings attendant upon God (as in Gen. 28:10–22, the story of Jacob's ladder). Sometimes an angel is the intermediary between man and God. He brings God's help, proclaims a message from God, or bears man's petition to God.

Later writings mention several special orders of angels, archangels and seraphim. Particular ones are given names: Gabriel, Michael. These heavenly beings are shining creatures with blazing eyes and covering wings. They become symbols for the glorious majesty of God. (See Isa., ch. 6, and Luke, ch. 2.) In The Revelation to John there is a picture of the final triumph of Christ. The scene is filled with adoring angels, heavenly attendants who wait upon the exalted Lord.

The Sadducees, a Jewish religious group who lived in the time of Jesus, did not believe in angels at all. The New Testament, however, retains the popular belief in angels as unseen spirits sent to guard and serve (see Acts 12:15;

Heb. 1:14). An ancient liturgical prayer says, "With angels and archangels, and with all the company of heaven, we laud and magnify thy glorious name." These words link the church on earth with the unseen world.

ANTICHRIST In its simplest sense, this word refers to someone who is against (*anti*) Christ. Antichrist is the one who denies that Jesus is the Christ (Messiah). He tries to break Christ's power by pretending to be divine and tempting the followers of Jesus to forsake their faith and deny their Lord. He is Satan, the evil one. (See SATAN.) In New Testament writing it is assumed that he will appear and do his work just before the final return of the Messiah in glory.

Because of this understanding of Antichrist, the church has tended to wonder if each time of terror and persecution, with a falling off of believers, indicated the close of the present age and promised the final coming of Christ. In the three letters of John this power is identified with those who lead Christians into false beliefs. In The Revelation to John the Roman emperor is identified with Antichrist because he persecutes and seeks to destroy the church and all that it stands for.

During the nineteen centuries of the life of the church, Antichrist seems most often to be used to describe a form of government (or heads of government) that puts itself in opposition to that which the Christian faith holds sacred. In the present century the Nazi Government in Germany persecuted the church and put its leaders in prison, and some Christians called Hitler the Antichrist. For many years the Communist Government in the Soviet Union has tried actively to turn people against the Christian faith, and its successive leaders have been labeled "Antichrist."

In a deeper sense, Antichrist is never a specific human person or even a particular system. Rather, it is the spirit in the world that convinces men that they can live without God, that they are themselves the creators and rulers of the world, and that by their own efforts they can build a perfect society. That spirit has no need for Christ. Indwelling persons and systems, it seeks to thwart the purposes of God and his rule.

APOCALYPSE An apocalypse is a writing that sets forth a vision of final events, usually in terms of destruction and judgment. An apocalypse is usually spoken or written in a time of distress. Zechariah was written during the Babylonian exile, Daniel during the Greek conquest. In vivid, symbolic language they pictured a final judgment in which the Holy God would punish those enemies of his people who had tried to keep them from serving him, and in which God's own people would be comforted and rewarded for their faithfulness.

The New Testament also contains apocalypses. There is one in Mark, ch. 13, where Jesus warns his disciples of coming distress and persecution. Matthew 25:31–46 describes the coming of the Son of man. Those who served others in the name of Christ would dwell with God, whereas those who had been indifferent would be thrown into "outer darkness."

The most elaborate apocalypse is that in The Revelation to John. The temptations, trials, and agonies of the faithful followers of Christ are described under several images. Finally, God judges all men, sends the persecutors and conquerors into outer darkness, and calls his own people into everlasting light and life in his holy presence.

An apocalypse is puzzling to the modern reader until he knows when it was written, to whom, by whom, and why. Then he realizes that if one is writing (as the early Christian writers were) to people whom the state considers suspicious, one cannot write plainly. The writer cannot say: "The Roman Empire is evil, but be strong; God will deliver you and will destroy the Empire." That would only get his readers into more trouble! So he says that Babylon was evil and caused great suffering, but God overthrew her and saved his people. "So shall Babylon the great city be thrown down with violence, and shall be found no more." (Rev. 18:21.)

An apocalypse is a message of hope to people in despair. When the church is safe, it does not hear such a message. When it is in trouble, an apocalypse like The Revelation to John provides strengthening in Christian faith.

APOCRYPHA The Apocrypha are a group of writings not found in the accepted (canonical) list of Biblical books. There are both Old Testament Apocrypha (to which the term "Apocrypha" when used alone usually refers) and apocryphal writings from the earliest period of the Christian church. At first the term referred simply to books that had been put aside because they were worn out or imperfect. Then it came to mean books that were not considered readable in public. Later, Apocrypha came to refer to books supposedly disclosing hidden teachings or mysteries. Since there are no such teachings in Judaism or Christianity, the word designated heretical writings, those whose teachings were contrary to generally accepted beliefs. Eventually the Apocrypha became a group of respected writings but were not included among the sixty-six books designated as Holy Scriptures.

The apocryphal writings from the New Testament period had as their intent filling in gaps in the New Testament story or furthering ideas that were not generally acceptable in the church. They are filled with legends and have a popular appeal. The decision of the church to leave these writings out of the New Testament, when the twenty-seven books were determined, indicates that even at an early date they were considered to be seriously lacking as sources for understanding the gospel or knowing the historical facts of the earliest church.

The Old Testament Apocrypha also contain legends, the purpose of which is to portray faithful Jews under injustice or persecution. There are Tobit, a pious man; Susanna, a wife saved from false accusations; Judith, who killed the foreign conqueror of her people; the Song of the Three Children in the Fiery Furnace; Bel and the Dragon. There are also reflective books of wise sayings: The Wisdom of Solomon and Ecclesiasticus. There is a book of prophecy, Baruch; and an apocalypse, II Esdras. There are three books of history: I Esdras, a continuation of the events narrated in Ezra and Nehemiah, and I and II Maccabees, a history of the struggle of the Jewish people against their Greek rulers, 175–153 B.C.

While a few of these books were originally written in Hebrew, the language of the Old Testament (I Maccabees, Tobit, Judith, Ecclesiasticus), the others were probably first written in Greek, a language with which many Jews were familiar. Their importance lies in the fact that they reflect the life, ideas, types of writing, and history of the centuries between the close of the Old Testament and the opening of the New Testament. The reader sees the heroism of a people who were faithful in spite of the efforts of foreign conquerors to force another religion upon them. This pressure had become intense under the Greek rule, resulting in the successful revolution under Judas Maccabaeus.

The list of books to be included in the Holy Scriptures of the Old Testament was officially decided about the year 90 at the Council of Jamnia. The place of the Apocrypha among the Jews has never been clear. The Christian church has kept the Apocrypha as a separate collection, useful for study and reading at times, but not essential for doctrine. For centuries they were used along with the Old Testament for readings in church services. At the time of the Reformation a definite stand was taken regarding them. Most of the Protestant churches set aside the Apocrypha for optional use; the Roman Catholic and Anglican Churches continue to use selections from the Apocrypha in the required lessons for services. Usually the Apocrypha are bound into Roman Catholic editions of the Bible. In most Protestant editions they are either omitted or bound separately. The Revised Standard Version of the Bible is available in a one-volume edition containing them.

The Apocrypha highlight a period of religious history that is too often neglected: the centuries immediately before the coming of Christ, the time of the preparation for his coming.

APOSTLE   The word "apostle" means "one who is sent forth." The word "missionary" means the same. ("Apostle" is derived from the Greek language; "missionary," from the Latin.) An apostle is a messenger, for he is sent to proclaim good news. But he is not sent forth merely to give his message and return. He is sent to show the message in his life: to heal, to help, to live among people, to suffer, and to die if necessary.

One is called to be an apostle. He does not simply choose to be one. The New Testament tells how Jesus called twelve men to be his disciples (learners) and later sent them out to teach and heal. (See Mark 3:13–19; 6:7–13.) When they returned, they told him how people had heard the message and how they had responded to the healing. The closing paragraph of Matthew's Gospel tells how the risen Lord appeared among the remaining Eleven, commanding them to go into the whole world, preaching, teaching, baptizing in his name; and promising to be with them "to the close of the age" (see Matt. 28:16–20). The first apostles were those, called and sent, who knew their Lord during his earthly ministry and on whom, in a very special way, the foundations of the church's life rest. Paul, who saw the risen Christ later, felt that he too was called to be an apostle.

There is a sense in which all Christians are apostles. Each has been called as a follower of Christ, and all are commanded to tell the good news of God's love in Christ. They do this wherever they live, wherever they work, and to all whom they know. Clergymen are apostles: they preach the gospel every Sunday. Missionaries are apostles: they go to far places to tell others about God's love. *Every* Christian is an apostle, and the church continues as each takes his call seriously.

See DISCIPLE.

ARK OF THE COVENANT   The word "ark" is first used in the Old Testament to refer to the boat which in time of flood saved one family that had been faithful to God's commands. After the Flood, God made a covenant (agreement) never again to destroy his people that way. (See Gen., chs. 6 to 9.)

The word "ark" is more frequently used to refer to the Ark of the Covenant, as described in the book of Exodus. The Hebrew people had stopped at the foot of the holy mountain, Sinai, while journeying from Egypt to their homeland of Israel. They had renewed with God the covenant that he had made hundreds of years earlier with their ancestor Abraham. They had written his law on tables of stone. Then they built a tent of meeting, or tabernacle, to remind them of God's presence. (See Ex., chs. 25 to 27.)

The Tables of the Law were placed in the Ark and kept in the Tabernacle. The Ark itself was an oblong box, ornamented with two golden angels. The box had four handles, so that two men, one at the front and one at the back, could carry it when the people moved forward on their journey. It was a sacred object signifying the presence of God.

Years later, when they were settled in their homeland, the Ark was kept at a holy place. It was always carried before their army in battle. Once when it was captured they became terrified and lost the battle. Not until many years later, during the time of King David, did they regain the Ark. His son, King Solomon, built a temple to house it.

Eventually, mention of the Ark disappears from the Biblical writings. It can only be surmised that it was destroyed when the Babylonians took the city of Jerusalem and destroyed the Temple in 586 B.C.

ASCENSION   The ascension is the event recorded in the New Testament as the last time at which the risen Christ was seen among his disciples. As such it marks a turning point in his relationship to his people.

After his death, Jesus was raised up by God and was seen among the disciples, and he talked with them on various occasions: at the tomb, in the upper room, by the Lake of Galilee. But this companionship was not to continue indefinitely. One day he appeared and spoke to them for the last time. He commanded them to preach the good news. He promised to send his Holy Spirit to enable them to fulfill this work, and told them to stay in Jerusalem until this power from God came upon them. Then he disappeared from their sight.

After this occasion the disciples lived in a new relationship to him. He was no longer their teacher but the risen Lord, returned to the glory of his Father. Thus Ascension Day has a particular place in the Christian calendar. It indicates that the Easter season is drawing to a close. It reminds the church each year that Christ the Lord is not only risen from the dead, but that he is exalted above all in the Heavenly Kingdom. The work of his earthly life has been completed on the cross. He has taken up again his divine life. As the disciples were reminded by the young man in white when they stood looking up into the heavens on that ascension day, "This Jesus, who was taken up from you into heaven, will come in the same way as you saw him go into heaven" (Acts 1:11).

ATONEMENT "To atone for" means "to make amends." It is the way in which broken relationships are healed. This happens every day. Someone (deliberately or by accident) hurts another person: breaks an object precious to him, hits him, or speaks sharp words. Then he sees the effect of this action and is sorry. "I wish I hadn't done this. What can I do to mend matters?" he says. If the person who has been hurt is willing to receive amends and not be resentful, the relationship is restored.

This also happens in the relationship between God and human beings. In fact, since God who is holy and loving desires and commands this kind of response from his children, the relationship is always being broken; for people prefer to do as they wish rather than to serve God faithfully and lovingly. They know how they should live, but they are unable to live that way. In short, man cannot save himself.

What should God do? He might say, "It does not matter, because I love you." That would assure men of his love, but make them very uncertain of his holiness and his justice. One can hardly be sure that the world is on the side of righteousness if men do evil and continue to seem good to God. How, then, can both justice and love survive together? Only if God himself has suffered for man's sin and through this action has drawn men to himself! So God came to live among men in the person of Jesus Christ. His suffering and death represent the suffering that sin brings to all men. Because death could not hold him, the resurrection is God's announcement that life is stronger than death, that healing is beyond suffering, and that righteousness is conqueror over sin.

Since that event, innumerable people, hearing the story and seeing God in Christ, have been moved by such love to be sorry for their sin. They have thus been able to know God's forgiveness, reconciliation, and a new kind of life. Only God's righteousness can enable his people to love and serve him faithfully. (See RECONCILIATION; RIGHTEOUSNESS.)

The Christian church has tried to explain this whole action of God as the doctrine of the atonement. Some have said that by his death, Christ ransomed man from the power of evil. By taking the evil upon himself, he "paid the price" for the children of Adam who had sold themselves to the evil one. Others have said that in his death Christ was substituted for each of us who ought to suffer because we have failed in the righteousness by which the children of God should live. As our substitute, he took our sins on himself so that we could be released from sin. Others have said that by the example of his death—suffering when he was not guilty—he sets us an example, and makes it possible for us to suffer and to live righteously.

All these explanations of what happened on Calvary are ways of saying that sin is so serious that God himself, because he is righteous as well as loving, cannot merely act as if it did not exist. He can forgive and restore his children by overcoming sin. This he does *for* them, since he alone is righteous, and they cannot do it for themselves. The good news of the gospel is that when a person participates in the death and resurrection of Christ, he repents, is forgiven, and has eternal life. This is the life of the Christian, and the life which the Christian church proclaims to all the world.

See REDEMPTION; SALVATION.

AUTHORITY Authority is power. A person in authority is one who can command others and they obey. In Biblical understanding, God alone holds complete authority. All human authority is derived from him and is granted by him. The person who holds authority over any part of God's creation—land, animals, or other people—does so as a steward. God will require an accounting from him as to how he has used his power. Paul indicates this: "Let every person be subject to the governing authorities. For there is no authority except from God, and those that exist have been instituted by God" (Rom. 13:1).

Inevitably there will be persons who exercise authority for selfish ends. Thus power becomes evil. The Christian must decide when to submit to such power and when to rebel. Man is a creature always in rebellion against his Creator, wanting to rule himself. It is easy to see how, when he has authority, he would think of its being absolute.

The question of religious authority arises within the church. Catholic groups believe that Jesus transferred his authority over his pepole to the apostles and, through them, to their successors. Since the bishops are considered to be these successors, they have traditionally been the authority that decides on Biblical interpretation, doctrine, and liturgical practice. In recent Roman Catholic teaching the pope has become the final authority on the definition of dogma (beliefs required of the faithful). The pope has pronounced new dogma only twice since 1870, when he was declared infallible on questions of faith and morals.

The Protestant Reformers rejected the doctrine of the succession of apostolic authority through the bishops. They insisted that the authority of the Twelve was unique. They placed religious authority in the written words of the Bible. Realizing that these words were capable of varying interpretations, they affirmed that the Holy Spirit would inspire with understanding those who looked to the Scriptures for the word of God.

The various branches of the Christian church have never agreed as to who has the authority to decide right beliefs (or their interpretation) or what constitutes Christian living. They are especially reluctant to cast out of the church those who differ from general norms. The Roman Catholic Church, however, exercises the right to excommunicate (that is, keep from the Holy Communion) members who refuse to accept a doctrine or who, in their lives, break the moral code. Some Protestant groups also exercise this right, either through the membership of a local congregation or through a wider jurisdiction.

Authority is not a privilege but a responsibility that the church holds under God in order that the members may be stewards of the gospel of Christ and witnesses to his work.

See OBEDIENCE.

B

BAPTISM   Baptism is the rite by which a person becomes a member of the Christian church. John the Baptist practiced it, calling on people to repent and be baptized as a sign that their sins were washed away and that God would deliver them from judgment and punishment. After John's death, the disciples of Jesus continued the practice. The Acts of the Apostles and the epistles indicate that baptism was a regular practice in the early church.

For the young Christian community, under the leadership of a risen Lord, baptism took on meanings beyond that of a washing away of sin. Going down into the water became a sign of going down into death with Christ. Rising from the water became a sign of receiving eternal life in him. So the rite of Baptism became the sign of entrance into the Christian life and the Christian community, the assurance of eternal life with Christ. It could be granted only to those who, responding to the story of the life, death, and resurrection of Christ, were sorry for their past life and wanted to live a new life in him. It came as a seal of the personal confession of Christ as Lord. It followed the promise of obedience and faithfulness to him until death, and it gave the assurance of his living presence to enable the believer to fulfill what he had promised. Customarily, in New Testament times, baptism was immediately followed by the "laying on of hands," which was the sign of the gift of the Holy Spirit, the Strengthener. Thus those who were baptized lived "in Christ," for his Spirit lived in them.

As time went on, variations in the rite appeared. Children were baptized because Christian parents wanted them to participate as members in Christ. The laying on of hands became "confirmation," and was an activity of the bishop (as it had earlier been of the apostles). Since bishops had wider geographical responsibilities because of the growth of the church, this rite was administered less frequently (see CONFIRMATION).

The preparation for Baptism became a serious one after Christianity began to make more converts among the pagans than among the Jews. The people scattered throughout the Roman Empire had no knowledge of God as he is known in the Bible. Catechumenal instruction was a long and serious work. ("Catechumen" is the name given to those willing to confess Christ and prepare for Baptism.) Baptism was customarily held on Easter, the day of Christ's resurrection.

Today there are Christian groups who baptize infants, requiring that the personal confession, made at the age of decision, be the final seal of entrance into the life of the church. Other groups withhold Baptism until a confession of faith can be made by the individual. These groups have continued the ancient practice of baptizing by immersion (that is, lowering the person completely under the water and bringing him up again). Some Christian bodies permit Baptism either in that form or in the modifications known as "sprinkling" or "pouring." In "sprinkling," the clergyman dips his hand into water and places it upon the head of the one to be baptized. In "pouring," a small quantity of water is poured from a pitcher over the head of the person. These forms are more generally used in baptizing infants, although the Eastern Orthodox Churches baptize the infant by immersion.

Whatever the method or whenever the time, Baptism names one as a Christian. Thus the name given the person in Baptism is his Christian name, the personal name, by which he is known to God. Many Christians, in time of trouble, have found new strength by saying to themselves, "I am a baptized Christian." They know that although all people are created by God, they belong to God in a new and special relationship by their baptism into Christ. This is their adoption to be children of God.

See ADOPTION; CONFIRMATION; SACRAMENT.

BEATITUDES A particular series of sayings of Jesus found in two forms and in two places in the Gospels is called the Beatitudes. As popularly known and often memorized, they are the opening section of the Sermon on the Mount, a collection of Jesus' teachings that begins with Matt. 5:1–12. Another version is found in Luke 6:20–26.

These sayings get their name from the opening word of each sentence, "Blessed are . . ." completed by the specific promise of the blessing. Thus the first says, "Blessed are the poor in spirit, for theirs is the kingdom of heaven" (Matt. 5:3). Luke reads, "Blessed are you poor, for yours is the kingdom of God" (Luke 6:20).

In these Beatitudes, Jesus addresses his disciples. In the Bible, "blessing" means the active, outgoing grace and goodwill of God. He promises that God is blessing the poor, the sorrowful, the meek, those desiring righteousness, the merciful, the pure in heart, the peacemakers, and those who are persecuted. These are promised that they shall see God, be called his children, inherit the earth, and inhabit the Kingdom of God. These sayings accept the difficulties that are a part of human life. They promise that God will comfort his own in their suffering, enabling them to be pure, merciful, and peaceful in spite of all things, and granting them the gift of his Kingdom.

Notice that this is not a teaching which is given to all men and in all the world. It is a teaching for disciples of Christ—those who have been redeemed by God. Jesus did not say that everyone would be able to live in this way, but only those who, in a special way, were the children of God. The Beatitudes are a picture of the Christian life in the world. They show how Christians witness to their faith in the world. They recognize that persecution may happen, but promise also the continual presence of God.

See BLESSING.

BELIEF Belief is the action by which one accepts something as true. To believe is a purposeful activity in which not only the mind but the whole person considers a proposition or an action and decides on its truth in relation to himself.

There are propositions of fact. To say that two plus two equals four is simply to recite a proposition in the form of symbols. It is accepted without thought or proof, for one has already accepted a meaning for "two" and "four." To say that one city lies a certain distance from another is a matter of fact, for it can be demonstrated by reliable forms of measurement. These facts lie in the realm of the objective. They are not important to life of themselves but only in relation to other facts. For example, the distance between two cities is important to the person who has to make the trip.

There are propositions of truth. These do not necessarily arise from data that can be proved in an objective way, but they may be of serious importance to the decisions of life. Thus the statement, "There is a God," cannot be proved in any such complete way as the earth can be proved round. It can only be demonstrated by saying, "See the order in the universe, the sense of law, the very existence of life." But this will not convince everyone that the world does not run by itself. Proving that God is love is even more difficult in the face of suffering and evil. This can never be more than the assurance by those who say, "We have known him to be love in spite of all the suffering and evil in the world." It can only be shown in terms of the Biblical story: God's goodness toward his people Israel, who have survived in spite of great suffering; God's triumph over evil in the crucifixion and resurrection of Jesus Christ.

So the Christian does not say, "I believe *about* God." That would simply mean that he thinks God exists, but that the fact of God's existence does not necessarily matter. He says, "I believe *in* God." This means that belief makes a difference in his relationship to God, to himself, and to other people. Belief *in* requires not only the assent of the intellect, but the assent of the whole self. To say, "I believe" is to say, "I have faith in."

Belief, then, cannot come simply by hearing a story or by memorizing some facts. It cannot even come by accepting as true that which another person says he has found to be true. The truth about God can be accepted in this way when one is small, but a time comes when each person must make this knowledge a part of his own life. This is belief that matters. It is the kind of belief that the early baptismal statements meant. The person about to become a Christian was asked, "Do you believe that Jesus is the Lord?" When the person answered, "I do," he was saying that he was willing to live and die by that belief.

See DOCTRINE; FAITH.

BIBLE The word "Bible" comes from a Greek word mean-"books" or "library," for the Bible is made up of many writings or "books." Sometimes it is called "the Scriptures," which means "writings." "Holy Scriptures" means that these are special writings through which God has spoken to his people. For this reason, it is said that the Bible contains the word of God.

The earliest materials in the Bible began as oral traditions: stories, poems, laments, and prophecies. These were remembered for years by being spoken about before being incorporated into the larger writings that form the books of the Bible as we know them. The first collection of writings was probably made in the time of King David, about 1000 B.C., and included the early traditions of the people of Judah. A hundred years later, another collection was made with a particular interest in the traditions of the Northern Kingdom, Israel. Beginning in the eighth century B.C., the oral and written traditions of the prophets appeared: Amos, Hosea, Micah, Jeremiah, Isaiah. When the two Kingdoms were conquered and many of their people exiled to Babylon, a further group of writings brought together the Priestly tradition. These, with some prophetic writings from the exile and the memoirs of Ezra-Nehemiah, and the "Writings" (Job, Psalms, Proverbs, etc.), comprise the basic documents from which the Old Testament was later compiled.

The New Testament began similarly in the preaching of the apostles, who declared that God had saved his people and sent his Son, Jesus, to save them. The stories of his acts and the remembrances of his teachings were illustrations of this good news. The four Gospels took their shape from these materials. The Acts of the Apostles tells the story of the first Christian communities. The letters were written for specific churches or groups of churches. The Revelation to John is addressed to churches under persecution.

The Bible is the written word through which God makes himself known. It shows how he has made himself known in the history of his people Israel. It describes his dealings with them under the covenant. It tells how he saved them in times of crisis and restored them when they had been faithless to him but later repented. This is called "holy history," for it is the action of God in the history of a nation. It includes the Law, the way of life given to God's people, through which they could serve him obediently.

The New Testament is the story of how God made himself known in Jesus Christ. The Word of God, which had already appeared in historical action, in the Law, in the words of the prophets, now appeared in a Person in whom the fullness of God dwelt.

The Bible arose from a religious community, who put into words what God had done for them, what he commanded of them, his promises and their response. At the same time, the life of the community was formed by these words of Scripture. They believed that God had chosen them to proclaim his mighty work and to witness in their life to what he had done. The Bible is central in Christian worship. The study of the Bible is important both to the individual Christian and to the church gathered together to hear the Word preached or to study it in groups. The promises and commands of the Bible are binding upon the church, which proclaims this to the whole world.

The Bible speaks to men today through the action of the Holy Spirit. God addresses man through the words of the Bible, calling him to faith and obedience. Many read but do not hear this call. When they read with a readiness to know it as God's Word, the action of the Holy Spirit enables them to interpret this Word in terms of their own life. So the Bible speaks to the individual, the church, and the world, calling to repentance and a new relationship with God.

See WORD OF GOD.

BISHOP The office of bishop is found in many parts of the Christian church, notably in the Roman Catholic, Eastern Orthodox, Anglican (Protestant Episcopal in the U.S.A.), Lutheran (Swedish and German, for example), Methodist (U.S.A.) and derivative denominations. Not all these bodies interpret the office in the same manner, though they use the same term.

The New Testament is unclear as to the details of the office in the earliest church. The word "bishop" is a translation of the Greek *episkopos,* which means "an overseer" (one who has oversight, watches over). The word suggests the figure of the shepherd who takes care of the flock in every need. (See Acts 20:28.) The bishop is likened to Christ, the Shepherd. His function is pastoral (pastor means "shepherd"). Several references seem to indicate that in each congregation there were a group of leaders who were both bishops and presbyters (elders). (See I Peter 5:1–4; Phil. 1:1.) Possibly several from among the elders were bishops and had special functions. By the beginning of the second century one person emerged as chief minister in each church. This is already indicated in Titus 1:5–7 and in I and II Timothy. Eventually his responsibilities covered an area rather than merely one church.

As the title suggests, the bishop was a person with administrative responsibilities. He made sure that the sick and needy were cared for by the deacons; that preaching, teaching, and evangelizing were carried on; that the Lord's Supper and other services were held. He was responsible for seeing that the tradition from the apostles was handed down faithfully to the second and third generations of Christians now arising. These were people throughout the cities of the Roman Empire who had little or no Jewish background and to whom the events in the life of Christ, fifty years earlier, were but words from the past. They were the heirs and successors to the apostles who had held a unique respect and authority in the first generation of the church's life. They symbolized the ongoing work of the Twelve. For this reason they became the ones to ordain men for the ministry of the church. The laying on of hands that followed baptism had been done by the apostles; now, in subsequent years, this was carried on by the bishops.

Bishops were chosen by the church for special service. But in a deeper sense the call to that office, as to the Christian life itself, has always been regarded as a gift of the Holy Spirit.

See PRESBYTER.

BLESSING A blessing is the grace of God given to man. The blessed are those to whom God grants his goodness. "To bless" means "to impart the grace of God." In the Old Testament the blessing of God was thought to be made known in terms of wealth, happiness, and long life. It was assumed by some of the writers of the psalms that those who did God's will and kept his law would be blessed by him and have prosperity (see Ps. 1).

As the Beatitudes indicate (Matt. 5:1–11), Jesus by his words gave another meaning to blessedness. Those who were poor, sorrowful, or persecuted for his sake were among the blessed, even though in the eyes of men it seemed as if God had turned against them. Their blessing would not be known on earth, but God had given them the Kingdom. They were blessed in that they belonged to God. His presence in their midst was the sign of his blessing, known only to them. (See BEATITUDES.)

The blessing was imparted by men, but only as the representatives of God. The words might be spoken by priest, prophet, or apostle, but it was always a prayer that the grace of God might come upon those who were blessed.

The blessing is completed when man blesses God, for in this the blessing returns to him who gives it. Thus Zechariah prays, "Blessed be the Lord God of Israel" (Luke 1:68), and Paul writes, "Blessed be the God and Father of our Lord Jesus Christ" (II Cor. 1:3).

The blessing upon food at the beginning of a meal is a blessing of God who gives food from the earth; it is an acknowledgment of his goodness to his children. The blessing also concludes a service of worship, and is the assurance to those who have been together that the grace of God goes with them into their everyday life, assisting them to be faithful to him.

See GRACE.

BODY Most people are sure that they know what "body" means: it means "flesh." But it also means something more. The body is flesh, soul, self, personality. It is not the whole person, but it gives form to the person. Notice that in referring to "body" one uses the pronoun "it," whereas in referring to a person one says "he" or "she." The body is living because of the living self.

In Biblical thought the body of flesh is important. The Bible knows nothing of disembodied spirits. God made a material world, and saw that it was good. The spiritual quality in Biblical thought is related to the material, and is not known apart from it.

This means that in the Bible people do not seek to be spiritual by denying the flesh or trying to escape from the things of earth. Rather, the spiritual is fulfilled in the earthly. The use made of the flesh spiritualizes it. So the body is good; it is the dwelling place of the Holy Spirit. He is known only in the flesh and not in any disembodied form.

This is why the Christian finds the fullest expression of the understanding of God as having been made known to men in a human being, Jesus of Nazareth, who was both God and man.

The body, then, includes the whole self. The person is made known in the flesh, even as God made himself known in the flesh. The self is made by God, indwelt by his Holy Spirit, and is therefore made sacred by him. The New Testament speaks also of a "spiritual body" (I Cor. 15:44), which will supersede the earthly body. It is in the body—earthly or spiritual—that God's creative work is known and the person's eternal life fulfilled.

The Bible speaks further of the church as the "body of Christ" (Eph. 4:12). The church, too, is an outward form through which the Holy Spirit works. The community of Christian believers constitutes the body that shows forth the work of Christ in the world.

See Soul.

BROTHERHOOD The term "brotherhood" refers to any group of people who consider themselves bound together as brothers. Some colleges have clubs that are called "fraternities," from the Latin *frater,* meaning "brother." In any such brotherhood the members have responsibilities toward one another as if they were members of the same family, promising to work together and to care for one another.

Brotherhood has a wider meaning. Some people have spoken of the whole world as a brotherhood, because all people are created by God and are, in that sense, God's children. As God, the Father of all, loves his children, so the children should love and care for one another.

The early Christians knew that they were bound to one another in Christ. They cared for one another as an expression of devotion to him. This was especially marked in times of suffering. However, as the church has grown, this bond has often been forgotten. Christians have not always remembered to be brothers to one another. When countries have been separated by war, Christians on either side have felt separated from the others. When Christians have faced tensions because of differing beliefs, they have often been brutal toward one another. On other occasions they have been separated by race, poverty, or education. Such separations indicate disobedience and unfaithfulness to the command of Christ that his followers love one another.

Christians are not only to love one another, but they are to have a loving concern for everyone in the world. This concern does not arise simply because God created all men, but because he has redeemed them. It comes because every Christian must know that Christ died for each person who has ever lived. This makes each person precious to God. Thus each person ought to be precious to God's people in the church.

This brotherhood is expressed in a willingness to permit each person to be himself, caring about people, and helping them according to their need and not because they act the way we want them to act. The Christian's concern demonstrates his faith to others. Many have said they were drawn to Christ because they have seen him in the lives of Christian people.

The Christian does not wait to show this concern until

people act the way he wants them to act. That would not be brotherhood, but only a desire to dominate others. The Christian is brother to all because if he takes his faith seriously, he cannot act in any other way. Brotherhood is an attitude toward other people by which a person is enabled to know that no one is strange or different, for all are created by God to love and serve him. All are so much loved by God that he sent his Son to live and die for them.

See FELLOWSHIP.

C

CATHOLIC The word "catholic" means "general" or "universal." A person who has broad international sympathies, who has read widely in the literature of many countries, or who appreciates food, music, and ideas from farflung places is referred to as a person of "catholic" tastes.

But in the Christian church the word early came to have a special meaning. At first there were only scattered little bodies of Christians in various cities of the ancient Greco-Roman world. However, instead of thinking of themselves as local church members only, they regarded themselves as members of the whole body of Christ. People worshiped and served together in local fellowships, but they felt that they belonged to the larger body of Christ no matter where they lived.

This understanding of the church was early interpreted by the theologians to mean the whole church, the total body of believers—hence "catholic" (universal). The church was not universal in the sense that there were churches everywhere in the world, though that too was to be the case many years later. At first the church was very small and was found in only a few places. What made the church catholic, or universal, was that God had acted in Jesus Christ to bring salvation to all mankind. The church was commissioned to spread the gospel of salvation to all mankind everywhere, for it was for all men that Jesus had been born, had lived, died, and been raised from the dead. Jesus was the world's Savior, even though many had never even heard of him. The task of the church was to make him known.

This meaning of "catholic" can be better understood by seeing how the Gospel of Matthew puts it. The risen Christ speaks to the apostles: "All authority in heaven and on earth has been given to me. Go therefore and make disciples of all nations, baptizing them in the name of the Father and of the Son and of the Holy Spirit, teaching them to observe all that I have commanded you; and lo, I am with you always, to the close of the age." (Matt. 28:18–20.)

The Apostles' Creed, used in the majority of churches, includes the clause, "I believe in . . . the holy catholic church." In some churches the word "universal" or "Christian" was substituted for "catholic" during the Protestant Reformation. That was in order to differentiate the Protestant Church from the Roman Catholic Church, since it had long been known as the "Catholic Church." In recent years it has come to be understood in all branches of the church that all Christians, whether Roman, Protestant, or Orthodox, belong to the whole church of Christ. The catholic church includes all believers, for Christ belongs to all. Where he is present, the church exists as one, holy, apostolic, and catholic.

See CHURCH.

CEREMONY   A religious ceremony is a way of carrying out a particular rite or sacrament. Ritual refers to the prescribed text of an act of worship. Ceremony refers to the manner in which the ritual is performed.

For example, the Lord's Supper (or Holy Communion) is an act of worship observed by almost all Christian bodies. The ceremony surrounding the Lord's Supper varies according to the different church traditions. In some churches the sacrament of the Lord's Supper is celebrated with great simplicity. The minister (in some cases an authorized lay-

man) presides at a table in the church, on which are placed
the bread and wine or grape juice. After a recollection of
the words of Jesus at the Last Supper with his disciples,
prayers are said; then the deacons (or elders) distribute
the elements to the congregation. In other churches the offi-
ciating minister uses more elaborate ceremony. This may
include placing his hands on the containers of bread and
wine when repeating the words of institution. The people
leave their places in the pews to go to the altar, where they
receive the consecrated elements.

Other acts of worship include many practices that are so
normal and regular that we seldom even think of them as
ceremonies. These would include such customs as bowing
the head while kneeling or standing for prayer; standing (or
sometimes sitting) for the singing of hymns; sitting during
the sermon while hearing about the meaning of the gospel
for life. The choir procession and recession and the gathering of the money offerings of the people are other examples
of ceremony.

Ceremony is rejected by some Christians as being artificial and unreal. Actually, however, some ceremony is necessary if there are to be recognizable ways of doing things.
Even the simplest service of worship (for example, a Friends'
silent meeting) consists of an ordered pattern that is accepted by the people as the agreed-upon way of doing
things. A ceremony is only a means to an end. If ever a
ceremony becomes an end in itself, cherished for its own
sake because it is beautiful or elaborate, there is a danger
that it can become artificial. But most churches find that
the proper use of ceremony provides a means whereby the
worship of God can be expressed with dignity.

See RITUAL.

CHARITY The question of relationships to other persons
is one that everyone has to face throughout life. Young
children learn early much about how to live with others
from dealing with members of their family and with other

persons who enter their lives. There are special times in life when some definite choice of a way of relationship must be made. Then the choices made will depend upon the way one really thinks about the meaning of persons.

The Jewish tradition always insisted that because God loves man, man can love God. It is impossible really to love God unless one shows charity toward one's neighbors. The meaning of charity is not merely to be "nice" toward other persons, but to regard them as fellow creatures, all of whom are dependent on God. The Old Testament laws require that help be given to all who need assistance: the weak, those lacking worldly means, widows, and orphans. Even the stranger, the foreigner who was not part of Israel, was to receive loving care: "When a stranger sojourns with you in your land, you shall not do him wrong. The stranger who sojourns with you shall be to you as the native among you, and you shall love him as yourself; for you were strangers in the land of Egypt" (Lev. 19:33 f.).

Jesus' teaching about charity toward others grows out of the Jewish background. When Jesus was asked by a scribe, "Which commandment is the first of all?" he replied that the first is "Love the Lord your God with all your heart, and with all your soul, and with all your mind, and with all your strength." He immediately went on to add that the second commandment is like the first: "You shall love your neighbor as yourself" (Mark 12:30–31). In other words, the way one acted toward neighbors must be an outgrowth of love toward God. ("Neighbors" are all with whom one comes in contact, even those who are not known personally but toward whom one must have attitudes and opinions.) This is made possible because of the enabling love of God: "We love, because he first loved us" (I John 4:19).

In other words, people do not just decide to be kind toward others. The other is one to whom God's love is shown. Each person in the world is one for whom Christ died. Each person is called to show to others the love that Christ has for all.

Charity is love in action. Those in whom the love of God dwells are true disciples of Jesus Christ and act toward others the way he acts toward all persons. This is sometimes called "the imitation of Christ." It does not mean trying to be exactly like Christ (which a human being cannot attain) but that his Spirit is always in those who are seeking to be his true followers.

Since the need for Christian charity is so great in the world, and each person can do this to only a limited degree, the church organizes its acts of goodwill. An example of Christian charity in action by the whole church is the type of relief work in many parts of the world made possible by money gifts to Church World Service of the World Council of Churches. That agency puts gifts into action wherever they are most needed, ministering to those in physical and spiritual need in behalf of the whole church. The continued gifts of many church people can be put to work efficiently and quickly in extending Christian charity to all in need.

See LOVE; STEWARDSHIP.

CHRISTIAN The earliest followers of Jesus Christ were known simply as those of "the Way." The Acts of the Apostles says that "in Antioch the disciples were for the first time called Christians" (Acts 11:26). The word "Christian" is also used in ch. 26:28.

To the Jews the term "Messiah" had always meant the anointed one of God who was expected to be the Savior. It was the conviction of Jesus' followers that he was the Messiah sent by God. The Greek translation of the Hebrew word for "Messiah" was *Christos*. When the gospel was carried into the Greek-speaking world, Jesus became known as "the Christ." The next step was for his disciples to be designated as Christians. Some scholars think the word is derived from another Greek word, *chrēstos,* which means "good" or "kindly." Since the Christians would not have referred to themselves in that way, probably the name was applied to them in the first years by non-Christians. The nickname stuck, and the word "Christian" gradually came to be used by Christians also in referring to themselves. The name was to be used by Jesus' followers for all time to come.

The term is used as an adjective in order to describe the ways in which Christianity applies to different practices and fields. Thus "Christian" theology refers to the various religious beliefs held by Christians. "Christian" ethics refers to the particular way in which Christians view ethics, and are called to understand their relationships to one another and to fellow human beings everywhere. "Christian" worship refers to the way in which people in the Christian church approach God in prayer and praise and practice its various rites and ceremonies.

The earliest Christians were conscious of having been called to a new depth and meaning in life because of what God had done for them in Christ. That is the reason why they originally thought of themselves simply as having been brought into a new way of life. Hence, they were followers of "the Way." First Peter was written to Christians being persecuted by the Roman Government. It is inspiring to realize that one of the three New Testament references to the term comes in that book: "Yet if one suffers as a Christian, let him not be ashamed, but under that name let him glorify God (I Peter 4:16). Christianity was expected to make a difference in their lives.

CHRISTMAS   When the church developed its calendar of worship, it was only natural that it would remember the great events associated with the life of Jesus Christ. The important thing for them was that God had come into the world in Christ, the Savior.

The first celebrations of the birth of Jesus were not limited to his birthday, but stressed his coming to be the Light of the World. The stories that grew up around the birthday of Jesus included both his birth in the stable at Bethlehem and the coming of Wise Men from the East (Gentiles), who recognized him not only as the Savior of Israel but of all mankind. The celebrations combined the birth and Epiphany (the showing forth of Christ to the Gentiles). In some parts of Christendom the Epiphany celebrations are still regarded as the more important festival, though in most of the Western churches the Nativity has come to be the one more generally celebrated.

The word "Christmas" means, literally, "Christ-Mass." It refers to the liturgy of the Lord's Supper (Mass), which came to be celebrated on Christmas Eve. Many churches observe the custom of having the Holy Communion on Christmas Eve or early Christmas morning, a reminder that the baby Jesus whose birth is remembered was the same one who would suffer death upon the cross for man's salvation. Some churches have other types of services on Christmas Eve or morning.

Many of the customs that have grown up in different nations around the Nativity celebrations are centered in the home or the community: Christmas trees, the giving and receiving of presents, and symbols such as the star, lights, wreaths, etc. Legends surrounding characters such as Saint Nicholas have developed into the personality and actions of Santa Claus.

When Christmas comes, joy reigns supreme in the hearts of those who welcome the Savior's birth. The carols and hymns of Christmastide spring out of the gift of God's love to the world in the Savior.

See ADVENT; EPIPHANY.

CHURCH Children learn to play a finger game that consists of interlacing the fingers downward between the palms and raising the index fingers up in a peak and crossing the thumbs in front of it. They say, "Here is the church, and here's the steeple;" then, opening the thumbs, continue: "open the doors, and here are the people!"

That childhood exercise points up a misunderstanding as well as a truth about the nature of the church. The misunderstanding is to think of the church as primarily a meeting place. The word "church" is used in that way, of course, to

refer to the houses for worship that the churches have constructed. Yet for many years after the beginning of the
Christian church, Christians did not have buildings of their
own in which to worship. They met in the Jewish synagogues
and in one another's homes. The truth in the finger game
lies in the emphasis it places on the *people* inside the church.
It is important to emphasize that the church is primarily a
congregation of persons, meeting for a particular purpose.

The church is not just another organization like a club or
fraternal order, chamber of commerce or labor union. It is
an organism rather than an organization—a company of
persons drawn together by the knowledge that God has
gathered them to fulfill his divine purpose for mankind. The
Jewish people had had a strong conviction of being the
people of God. The Christians continued to feel this way,
except that they were sure that God had acted anew in Jesus
Christ to declare his will for the world. Sometimes, therefore,
the church was referred to in the New Testament as the
"New Israel." The Greek word for church, *ekklēsia*, gives us
the English word "ecclesiastical." The church is the assem-
bly of the people of God called out in loyal obedience to
God as he has made himself known in Jesus Christ. It is
assigned the task of bringing the message of God's love to
all.

Sometimes the church is referred to as the "church militant." This describes the life of the church in the world as
it goes about doing its assigned tasks: proclaiming the gospel, administering the sacraments, and ministering to all
persons in the name of Christ. It is in a never-ending struggle against the forces of evil in the assurance that the final
victory belongs to God. The church militant must be organized for its work; to that extent it is an organization. This
is true both on broad denominational levels and in local
communities. Officers are elected with specific tasks to do;
commissions and committees are set up to plan and carry
out missionary, educational, and service aspects of the
church's life.

The way in which denominations are organized is called "polity." Because of various understandings of the nature of the church, its government is usually one of three types: (1) *congregational,* with the powers of government vested in the local church; (2) *presbyterial,* governed by a regional elective body known as the presbytery or synod; (3) *episcopal,* with the leadership vested in a bishop, who administers the spiritual and material affairs of a diocese.

The ecumenical movement of today is bringing churches of various backgrounds together in a fresh rediscovery of their oneness in Jesus Christ. Although traditions and practices differ, there is a growing recognition that Christians all belong to one another and need to witness to the world that they are one in Christ.

CHURCH YEAR The longest section of the four New Testament Gospels refers to the events of Jesus' ministry just before and during the last week of his life. Jesus' death and resurrection were central for the disciples. It was especially the details of those events that they kept uppermost in mind and finally wrote down.

Jesus' last days on earth were vivid in the recollection of the first Christians as they met for their weekly Sunday worship and broke bread together. Soon it became the regular practice of the church to remember Jesus' last meal with the Twelve. The very fact that they met on Sunday instead of Saturday was also a form of remembrance, for it was on that day (and not the traditional Sabbath) that the first Easter occurred.

The remembrance of Jesus' whole life and ministry gradually became a pattern by which the church organized its yearly life. It took many centuries for the detailed calendar of the Christian year to develop, but the movement in that direction started fairly early in the history of the church. Eventually a complete cycle of seasons was developed and repeated every year.

Although the calendar year starts with January 1, the

church year begins with the first Sunday in Advent, four weeks before Christmas. Advent is a period of preparation for the anniversary of Jesus' birth. It reaches its climax on Christmas Day. Christmas finally became set as December 25, although no one knows the exact date on which Jesus was born in Bethlehem. The season of Christmastide lasts twelve days, hence the traditions that have grown up around the "twelve days of Christmas." January 6 is observed as the Epiphany—the remembrance of the visit of the Magi (Wise Men) to the manger at Bethlehem. Traditionally they came from the East, which means that they were Gentiles (non-Jews) and their coming to adore the Christ-child symbolizes the fact that he is God's Savior for the whole world.

The date of Easter is a variable festival. Unlike Christmas, which is celebrated on the same date each year, Easter, the day of resurrection, is celebrated on the first Sunday after the first full moon following the spring equinox. Astronomers have been able to figure out the date of the vernal equinox, hence of Easter, for many years ahead. For example, in 1970 Easter will come on March 29; in 1980 on April 6; in 1990 on April 15; and in 2000 on April 23. It can fall as early as March 23 and as late as April 25.

In the early Middle Ages the church developed a period of preparation for Easter that came to be known as Lent. This consists of forty days, starting with Ash Wednesday. That name comes from an old custom. Penitents had ashes placed on their heads by the priest after attending Mass on the first day of Lent. The ashes came from burning the palms of the preceding Palm Sunday. During Lent, people usually follow special schedules of prayer and attend special devotional services in their churches. Lent reaches its climax in Holy Week, starting with Palm Sunday. Holy Week commemorates the events in the last week of Jesus' life on earth. Maundy Thursday (from the Latin *mandatum novum*, "new commandment": "A new commandment I give unto you") recalls the day the Last Supper was held, and Good

Friday, the day of the crucifixion, culminating in the joyous festival of the resurrection day.

Fifty days after Easter comes Pentecost, the day the Christians received the power of the Holy Spirit. Sometimes it is called the birthday of the church, though actually the church had already started with the company of Jesus' disciples during his lifetime. Pentecost was the name of a Jewish festival. Christians sometimes called this Whitsunday, because of the white robes once worn by those being baptized on that day.

The remainder of the Christian year centers in the day called Trinity Sunday and the many Sundays after Trinity. All the other seasons recollect actions of God in the life of Jesus. Trinity is a season of teaching about those things which pertain to what God *is* rather than to what he does— adoring him for himself as well as for his mighty acts.

See ADVENT; CHRISTMAS; EASTER; EPIPHANY; GOOD FRIDAY; LENT.

CIRCUMCISION Circumcision of male children developed as a religious rite among Jews. It was a reminder to them of their part in the covenant of God with the people Israel. It consisted of a ceremony during which a portion of the foreskin of the penis was removed by the priest or rabbi. This practice commemorated God's selection of the Jews to perform a special purpose in the world. The rite became part of the Law.

When Christianity grew out of Judaism, the practice of circumcision was reinterpreted with a purely spiritual significance. Paul wrote (Rom., chs. 3 and 4) that Abraham, the patriarchal father of the people of Israel, had been made righteous by God even though he had not been circumcised (for the rite had not yet developed in Abraham's time). He became the father of all succeeding persons of faith. Thus the only circumcision required of Christians was to be the circumcision of faith.

There was a party within the early church who insisted

that before one could be a Christian one had to undergo all the requirements of the Jewish law. It was decided by the Council of Jerusalem that the gospel was for all men and not merely for those who were first Jews.

See LAW.

COMMUNION OF SAINTS   One of the statements in the Apostles' Creed is this: "I believe in . . . the communion of saints." This follows immediately after the statement, "I believe in . . . the holy catholic [universal] church."

The meaning of "communion of saints" cannot be understood without thinking of the church. In one sense the church *is*—among other things—the communion of saints. In the New Testament letters the word "saints" is used to describe the members of the church in particular places. And "communion" is another word for the fellowship they have with one another within the community of the church. The title of the sacrament, the "Holy Communion," also uses this word, symbolizing their fellowship through a sharing of the common meal, in keeping with Jesus' institution.

However, "communion of saints" as a reference to the life of the members of the church goes more deeply than merely describing the organized church in a particular place where we may belong. We can distinguish between the visible church (with its clergy, membership rolls, buildings, groups, and so on) and the inner, spiritual church. The organized church is the means whereby the company of Christians express in their common life all those concerns and meanings that exist in the church regarded first as the body of Christ. The church in this sense includes not only the living but those who have been members of the church many generations previously. It embraces those who have responded to God's call from the beginning of time and all who will be in the church long after we are gone, to the end of time.

It is as participants in this communion of saints that Christians carry out God's purpose, remind one another of their common Christian tasks, hear the Word of God, and share in the sacraments.

See CHURCH; SAINT.

CONFESSION There are two distinct meanings of the word "confession" as it is used in the language of religion.

1. The term is used to describe the basic statements of doctrine as adopted by individual church bodies or groups of churches. Most of these confessions of faith grew out of special circumstances in history that required church groups to set forth clearly what they most surely believed. Disagreements often developed among church people—especially among theologians—as to the interpretation of important Christian views about God, Jesus Christ, the Holy Spirit, the church, the sacraments, the ministry, etc. Usually these differences became clear enough to the leaders of the groups, but the people who followed them wanted and needed guidance about such matters. Councils or conferences were held in which the differences were debated, and finally a complete statement of belief was drawn up and published.

These confessions should not be confused with creeds. Usually the confessions were long statements based on the articles of the ancient Apostles' and Nicene Creeds and interpreting them.

During the Reformation period a number of famous confessions of faith were drawn up, such as the Augsburg (Lutheran), the Heidelberg (Reformed), and the Westminster (Presbyterian), to mention only a few of the most famous. Various church policies and practices grew out of these formal confessions.

2. The word "confession" is also used in describing the attitude of Christians toward the sins they have committed. Because no one is spiritually perfect, everyone commits sins against God. These may take the form of personal pride and selfishness, or they may involve injury to a fellow human being. Jesus taught that God, the loving Heavenly Father, is always willing to forgive the sins of those who truly turn

toward him. Just as the Heavenly Father is forever merciful to men in forgiving their trespasses, so ought they to be willing to forgive one another. One cannot even know his sins until he looks deeply into himself, asking: "What have I done? Why did I do this?" Only then can one approach God, confessing one's sins and asking him for the cleansing and pardon he has promised.

Because all people sin, it is proper that when they are gathered in divine worship they should join in a common prayer asking God's forgiveness. This is usually a part of services of worship in the church. Speaking words from the Scriptures or from the liturgy, the minister pronounces the assurance of pardon (or absolution).

Protestants believe that God directly hears his people's prayers and grants his pardon without the intermediary help of a minister. Oftentimes, however, people with special problems and feelings of guilt over their sins find it helpful to see a minister privately. Ministers usually have specialized training and a deep pastoral concern for their people. They are able to help such persons realize the loving forgiveness of God, available to all his children. Ministers respect the confidences of those who come to them, and do not betray to others the sins that people confess before God in their presence.

In the Roman Catholic Church it is required that a communicant confess his sins in the presence of a priest at least once a year in order to receive the Holy Communion at Mass. This is called "auricular confession" (confession into the ear of the confessor). The priest does not forgive sins—only God can do that—but he is empowered by his ordination to mediate forgiveness in the name of Christ. Confession and absolution are regarded as the sacrament of penance.

God knows the hearts of men even before they approach him to confess their sins. But until they take the initiative to come before him in sincerity, truth, and a willingness to amend their lives, they cannot receive his help. He desires his children to live in company with him and as brothers with one another. Jesus taught that if anyone comes to worship but has done something wrong against another, he must go to the person he has wronged and make things right before his offering of worship can be acceptable before God.

See CREED; PARDON; REPENTANCE.

CONFIRMATION Candidates for Baptism in the early church were carefully screened and trained before they were admitted to this rite which made them members of the church. In some cases a person had to wait as long as three years to be baptized. It must be remembered that at first only adults were baptized; hence the emphasis on making sure that the candidates understood the seriousness of the step they were taking. (Scholars think that in some cases whole families were baptized together, but the evidence is not conclusive.)

Immediately after Baptism, a candidate passed through the rite of the laying on of hands by the bishop or chief elder. This ancient practice is referred to in several places in the New Testament. Baptism and the laying on of hands together made up the ceremony of initiation into the membership of the Christian church. In the course of time, the laying on of hands, usually reserved to the bishop, came to be separated from Baptism. As the church grew, the bishop had too many congregations under his care to permit him to be present at all instances of Baptism. The local parish clergy administered that rite, and the bishop would come once a year or oftener for the laying on of hands. In Eastern Orthodox Churches the parish priest administers the total rites of initiation in one service.

At the time of the Protestant Reformation confirmation (as the laying on of hands had come to be called) was abandoned for some years. Later it was restored in both the Lutheran and Reformed traditions. It came to be regarded as the rite by which a person who has been baptized in his infancy is admitted to adult status in the church and welcomed to the Lord's Supper. In the course of time most Protestant churches have come to use some service of admission to communicant status. Sometimes this is referred to as "joining the church." However, most churches recognize that Baptism makes one a member of the church.

The word "confirmation" means ratifying, or saying yes to, the vows that were made for one by parents or sponsors at the time of Baptism, or, in the case of a person baptized as an adult, of the vows he himself has made at his Baptism. It is the way of affirming before the church that he now purposes to take upon himself the whole responsibility of being a mature Christian and seeking to live in the world as a faithful follower of Jesus Christ as long as he lives. "To confirm" also means "to strengthen" and indicates the strengthening power of God's Holy Spirit renewed in the laying on of hands.

Confirmation is regarded as an important occasion. Young people usually attend a preparatory class, conducted by the minister, lasting for periods varying from two months to two years. Adult candidates, too, are usually required to attend a similar class. In these courses, the candidates for confirmation study the meaning of church membership, reexamine the doctrines of the church, find out together what is involved in being Christians in today's world, and reexamine the meaning of the Bible, prayer, and worship for their lives.

The actual confirmation ceremony includes, in some churches, the laying on of hands on each candidate's head, with a prayer that he may continue faithful and that God will strengthen him by his Holy Spirit. In some churches the laying on of hands is omitted but the minister and elders or deacons extend the "right hand of fellowship" to the baptized persons who are being admitted as communicant members of the church.

See BAPTISM.

CONSCIENCE　An old proverb says, "Let your conscience be your guide." That is still quoted from time to time, but what does it mean? Is there something within a person that can be called the "conscience"? If so, what and where is it?

"Conscience" comes from the Latin words for "to know" and "with," which can provide a clue to its meaning. With what shall one know? The answer comes from the Biblical understanding of man. The Biblical writers always insisted that a person is not just a body or just a mind. The whole person counts. When a person acts, his whole being is involved. When he makes a decision about a problem, the conclusion is not reached with the mind alone. The whole self has to agree if he is to act on the conclusion.

The ancients thought that the feelings could be located in particular parts of the body. Paul wrote that with the heart, man believes and is justified. (Rom. 10:10.) Today it would be generally agreed that the conscience—the knowledge of what is right and the willingness to act on the basis of that conviction—does not belong to any one part of the body. It is the whole mind-body that says yes or no, and a person acts "in one piece," so to speak.

The conscience can be said to be the sensitivity by which a person looks at his actions. A person without conscience is one who acts on the basis of impulse, purely selfish likes and dislikes. A person with a sensitive conscience, on the other hand, is one who asks whether he can perform this or that action without violating his own wholeness and without injuring other persons. The Christian believes that the Holy Spirit is the source of a good conscience, and that if one truly prays for help, he will discover the inner resources necessary to determine how to decide courses of action.

Oftentimes the conscience turns out to be pretty much a matter of the accepted values of the society in which one lives. Sometimes people act as they do, not because of any personal decision, but because certain standards of behavior are expected in the social groups in which they move. For example, many young people would be mortally worried about wearing red slacks if the prevalent custom were for the crowd to wear blue ones. The problem gets especially acute when matters of human relations, politics, or religion are concerned. For then, sometimes, people let their decisions be dictated by group behavior, whether right or wrong. Sometimes what the group insists on as right may be morally wrong. This is why Christians rely on the values and standards encouraged by the Christian community, the church, and work out together patterns of conduct that can truly reflect a Christian conscience.

CONTRITION "If we say we have no sin, . . . the truth is not in us." (I John 1:8.) The Christian knows that he is always a sinner standing in the need of God's forgiveness and grace. This does not mean, however, that the Christian has to go around wearing a mournful countenance. The heart of the gospel is that even if men cannot save themselves, God has acted in Christ to forgive their sins when they truly repent and turn to him.

Contrition is the state of being truly sorry for sin, along with having intention to persevere in avoiding sin in the future. Even before God's help is asked, he is at work within the person, making him want to face up to the true self that he is intended to be. When a person knows that all is not well, that he has wronged someone or done something that conscience says was not right, and if he is truly sorry, he will face his action and willingly repent. This is not just feeling sorry for what has been done. It is feeling sorry so completely that one is moved to do something about it in terms of a future course of action.

One of the traditional invitations to the Holy Communion reads as follows: "Ye who do truly and earnestly repent of your sins, and are in love and charity with your neighbors, and intend to lead a new life, following the commandments of God . . . : Draw near with faith." Then follows the prayer of confession.

For it is recognized that contrition precedes confession, as confession precedes forgiveness. Forgiveness brings that restoration with God which makes possible the intention of living a new life.

See CONFESSION; FORGIVENESS; PARDON; REPENTANCE; SIN.

CONVERSION No one is automatically a Christian. To be sure, one may be born into a Christian family, be baptized as an infant, be surrounded by church atmosphere from childhood. These facts do not guarantee that the Christian faith will become personally meaningful to him.

Some persons suddenly awake to a deep sense of relationship to God. The cause may not be obvious to them. Possibly it is the influence of a friend or pastor, the result of some crisis experience in which one has to make some decisions and knows that he needs help from outside himself. It may be the result of a renewed interest in prayer and the devotional life, or the word from Scripture or preaching that seems to be personally addressed to himself. The result is a turning away from one's former habits and a reliance on God's help. This is called "conversion."

A sudden conversion may not always be so sudden as it seems. Perhaps many influences have brought it to pass. Yet in this kind of conversion a person can usually point to a specific experience or time (or period of time) in which the conversion took place.

Others do not experience any such sudden conversion, but feel, rather, a gradual unfolding within them of relationship to God. They know that their life is entering deeper levels, clearer understandings, and firmer purposes. If anyone asked them to explain exactly what has caused this, they might not be able to say. Yet they know that prayer is now easier for them, life is more wonderful, and Jesus Christ becomes not just a great teacher but the very Lord of their existence. They find a new joy in the worship and activity of the church, which becomes their spiritual home.

There are examples of conversion in the New Testament Gospels. Some Galilean fishermen left their nets and followed Jesus, who promised that they should become fishers of men. Obviously they had a turn of heart, a conversion, for they willingly left all and followed him. (Mark 1:16–20.) The conversion of Saul of Tarsus is another example. (Acts 9:1–8.) Saul turned from being a persecutor of the Christians into being the most ardent disciple of all, Paul the apostle. Jesus himself had taught, "Unless you turn [that is, become converted] and become like children, you will never enter the kingdom of heaven." (Matt. 18:3.)

Conversion is not just what experience does to one or what others may urge one to do. It is the work of the Holy Spirit in the hearts of those who have faith toward God. It can happen at any age, and it may happen in a single person's life more times than one.

COVENANT The Hebrew religion is based on a covenant between God and man. The book of Exodus gives the setting of the original covenant. Having revealed himself to Moses, God gives him a special task to do: he is to lead his people Israel out of slavery in Egypt toward the Promised Land. This covenant was sealed on Mt. Sinai and was always looked back upon by the leaders of the Hebrews as the basis of their relationship with God. When the life of the people was renewed after catastrophe or when they were making a fresh start, it was in relation to a renewal of the covenant.

The whole history of Israel can be thought of as the story of the covenant. When the people were faithful to God, they were blessed. Whenever they forgot God, they were endangered and received punishment for their unfaithfulness. The prophets, such as Amos, Hosea, Ezekiel, continually reminded the people of the covenant. As Jeremiah puts it: "I will be your God and you shall be my people" (Jer. 7:23; 31:33). It was not an agreement started by the people. It is God who first approaches the people and calls them into the covenant relationship. He takes the initiative; the people respond by their faithfulness or unfaithfulness to his call and his guidance.

Sometimes the covenant was compared to a marriage. Israel is the wife, and even if she is unfaithful, God forgives and restores her when she returns. The rise of the monarchy under David and Solomon is interpreted also as a renewal of the covenant. The Torah (Law) as contained in the first five books of the Bible became the guidebook for the people.

The early Christians also were influenced by the covenant idea. It was their conviction that in the life and work of Jesus Christ, God had made a new covenant with the people, one that was not limited to Israel but was intended for all mankind. This was the covenant of God's love poured out completely for his people's salvation by Jesus' life, death, and resurrection. At the Last Supper of Jesus with his disciples he told them that he was making a new covenant with them.

The Christians thus began to think of themselves as the New Israel. They were the participants in the new covenant. In the course of time the Scriptures came to be thought of in these same terms. The Hebrew Bible came to be known as the Old Testament (or Covenant); the new writings, including the Gospels and epistles, as the New Testament (or Covenant).

The word is used in another sense by some church bodies such as the Baptists and the Congregationalists. They think of the church as constituting the people of Christ in any given place who bind themselves together into a compact, to worship and serve God. They reach an agreement together concerning a way of life and government for themselves in the church. This is sometimes called a covenant.

COVETOUSNESS   To covet something means to desire it to such an extent that a person cannot imagine himself as being happy if he should be deprived of the hope of getting what he wants.

Covetousness may refer to things or to persons. Sometimes a person wants a certain thing that another owns, or there may be other barriers in his way. Sometimes he desires to "possess" another person for his own use or enjoyment. Such a desire becomes so consuming a passion that all his thoughts are directed toward getting what he wants at any price. The same desire may be directed toward success, recognition, fame, or any other goal or ambition. This can operate in the lives of groups of people as well as in the lives of individuals. The result can be disastrous. Sometimes persons desiring certain ends will twist the truth, cheat, or even rob in order to get what they want.

The Ten Commandments prohibit covetousness. "You shall not covet . . ." (Ex. 20:17.) The mere hearing of this commandment will not change a person's motives, but it is a reminder that anyone who puts "inordinate desire" ahead of right relationships to people and things is acting contrary to the will of God.

In contrast to covetousness, Jesus taught that persons should seek first the Kingdom of God and his righteousness, and then all other things needful would be added to them. It is life in God's Kingdom that one should desire more than anything else.

CREATION   All early peoples sought to explain the world and how it came to be. In doing so, they developed myths or legends telling about the beginnings of things. The title of the first book in the Bible, "Genesis," means "Beginnings." In chs. 1 and 2 of that book there are two accounts of the creation of the world, the first telling in broad outlines of the beginning of the natural world, and the second emphasizing the beginnings of man. The important thing about these ancient accounts is that they attribute the origin of everything to an intelligent, purposeful God, who had in his own being the reason for making the world as it is. Furthermore, these accounts put an emphasis on man as the end of God's creation: that is, according to their beliefs God created the world in order that it might be the habitation of persons who could know and love him.

Sometimes the reader of these ancient accounts asks why they are so different from the explanations of the origin of the earth (and the vast universes beyond our own solar system) that are given by scientists today. The answer is that these Biblical materials were never intended to be scientific explanations. They were the efforts of people of faith to set forth their understanding of the ways of God with his world. They were written long before modern science was ever dreamed of. There is no real contradiction between modern physics and the Bible. The scientists are attempting to explain causes and results, whereas the Biblical writers were seeking to point to the God who is understood by faith.

Some ancient Gnostic myths declared that the world was made, not by the highest god or gods, but by an inferior, not completely intelligent deity. Others have said that once the world and its laws were established, the God who created it withdrew from the scene and simply let the world carry on by itself, a view that is called deism. Still others have said that the world *is* God, that there is no difference between the Maker and the processes that he set in motion; that is called pantheism.

Christianity is a religion of theism: that is, it not only identifies God as the Creator who made the world, but the One who continues to control its processes. The world is still in the hands of him who made it. He is greater than his creation, yet works through it, and has purposes for man whom he has placed in the world. Christianity teaches that history is important: God is an actor in the events of the world he made, and all that man knows about God has been revealed by God.

CREED A creed is a statement of faith. *Credo* (Latin) means "I believe." It does not mean "I believe *that*" so and so is true, but it means "I believe *in*." When we say, "I believe in God," we affirm that we put our trust in God, we turn to him, and are related to him in the deepest part of our existence.

The church developed creeds in order to enable its people to have statements or summaries of the Christian faith. They could repeat the creeds when they gathered together for worship, and when they sought to explain to those outside the church just exactly what were their distinctive Christian understandings.

In the early church there was not always a clear agreement about the beliefs that should be commonly held by Christians. Leaders of the church debated many questions. Probably at first the only "creed" was a simple statement such as was made by those desiring to be baptized: "I believe in Jesus Christ, the Son of God." The fuller understanding of God as he had made himself known in Jesus Christ was developed in the Apostles' Creed. Although this was not written by any of the original apostles, it contains the essence of the preaching of the apostles; hence, its name. It is the most widely used creed in the church. Another is the Nicene Creed, named for the city Nicaea, in which a famous council was held.

Some Protestant churches do not require their members to assent to any one creed. In most churches where the Apostles' and Nicene Creeds are used, the people have freedom to interpret the articles of the Creed according to their own best understandings. In some churches modern statements of faith have been composed. Very seldom is a creed used as a "test" for right belief. It is, rather, the expression of what the church most deeply holds to be true for all times and places, individual interpretation being necessary if the creed is to be a living guide to faith.

See BELIEF; CONFESSION.

CROSS First of all, the cross refers to the actual means used to put Jesus to death. Because of the hatred of the religious leaders toward him and the fears of the Roman governor as to what might happen in the state if Jesus were permitted to continue his preaching, false charges were raised against him and he was led from the judgment hall to die a cruel death on Golgotha outside Jerusalem. Crucifixion was the form of capital punishment used by Rome for only the lowest criminals. It was meant to inflict the severest physical pain on those condemned to die. Jesus was nailed to a cross erected between similar crosses on which two thieves were hanged. Soldiers mocked him. Even the vinegar on a sponge put up to his lips to moisten them was simply a prolonging of his agony.

The cross was not the end of Jesus' influence, but only the beginning. His followers were to know by the resurrection that men could not defeat God's purposes through Christ for the world. His Spirit would return to cheer, comfort, and inspire them to preach the gospel in all the world. They could not have known this power of the risen Christ unless first, as he had warned them he would, he died.

The Christian church has always remembered the cross as the sign of God's salvation. It became a cherished symbol for Christians from the earliest times. Eventually crosses would be placed on the altars of churches, and church buildings would be constructed in the shape of a cross. Hymns would recollect it and artists portray it. What had been the expected destruction of Jesus by his enemies became the source of power for those who followed the Savior in all the years to come.

D

DEACON The word "deacon" comes from a Greek word that means "to serve." Jesus used the word in saying that he came not to be served but to serve (Mark 10:45) and he called the Twelve to this kind of service. It means the regular work of a servant, specifically "to wait on at table."

In Acts, ch. 6, one reads that seven men were chosen by the people to help the apostles. They were set apart to their office with prayer and the laying on of hands. Their work was more than that of simple service, for Stephen preached as well as helped with the distribution of food to the poor.

The work of the deacon is mentioned in two other places

in the New Testament: Phil. 1:1 and I Tim. 3:8–13. In the former passage, the deacon is noted as one of the officers in a congregation. In the latter passage, the writer outlines the kind of person a deacon ought to be.

No one knows exactly when the many offices mentioned in the New Testament became narrowed to a few. Nor is it known at what point the selection of persons to fill such offices began to be made only by appointment. Early in the second century the deacon became the assistant or helper to the bishop, both in the conduct of worship and in general administration.

Today the office of deacon is still that of helper. In some churches, ordination to the diaconate is the first step in becoming a full clergyman. In other churches, the deacon is a lay person elected by the church who becomes a special helper to the minister in the work of the church, particularly in collecting and dispensing alms for those in need. The deacons, therefore, also help in missionary work. Since in the early days of the church, the people of the congregation brought the bread for the Communion as part of their offering, it is customary in some churches for the deacons to have charge of preparing and helping to serve the Communion. Hence, the office of deacon, variously interpreted, is looked upon in the church as one of high honor for which a man must be worthy and to which he is called.

DEATH   Death is the cessation of life and the necessary ending to every human life. But mankind has never believed that this was final. Man thought that in dreams his spirit could roam while his body lay quietly. His religious beliefs always included the hope that when his body lay in unwaking sleep, his spirit would still have life.

The Old Testament indicates a belief that the continuation of life lies in the continuity of the family that can remember a man across the years. When man is faced with the problem of early death, the Old Testament suggests that man has sinned. The story of the Garden of Eden (Gen., ch. 3) links the fact of sin with death.

But if God created man in his own image, to serve and love him, then death could not be part of God's plan. Sin and death separate man from God. Only God can save man by effecting a way to overcome such separation.

The Bible does not accept the view that each man has an "immortal spirit" which survives the death of the body. Eternal life, resurrection from the dead, is the gift of God. It is granted in the forgiveness of sin and the establishment of a new relationship to God.

If death is the penalty for sin, it is also the means of being saved from the power of sin. The death of Christ was brought about by the sinfulness of men. But God indicated his power over sin and death in the resurrection of Jesus. The forgiveness of sins overcomes the first death, which is separation from God. The Christian lives in a new relationship to God through the power of the Holy Spirit. He has eternal life now, and Baptism is the sign of this rebirth. He need not fear the second death, which is the death of the body. For he knows that God who has saved him from sin will also save him from death and bring him to the resurrection.

See BAPTISM; ETERNAL LIFE; RESURRECTION.

DISCIPLE The word "disciple" means a "learner." The rabbis (teachers) in Jesus' time had disciples, groups of men who gathered around them to study the Law. These disciples accepted and practiced the teaching of the rabbi who was their teacher. John the Baptist had disciples. Jesus gathered a group of disciples about him, but the inner circle consisted of those who are called the Twelve. These were with him most of the time, although sometimes he took aside only three who seemed to be special disciples: Peter, James, and John. The Gospels often refer to "his" disciples and this usually means the group who accompanied him in his travels, heard his teaching, and were being prepared by him to carry on his work.

In The Acts of the Apostles the word "disciple" refers to those who believed in Christ. The disciple learned from his master and was obedient to his master. He preached the good news that God had saved his people. He served others, as his master had done. He was faithful even under persecution, and when necessary, died for his Lord.

These characteristics have always been the marks of the disciple of Jesus. He learns of God through Christ and shares this love with others through his words and actions. Faithful through life, he expects one day to enter into the joy of his Lord.

See APOSTLE.

DISCIPLINE Because the Christian is a disciple of Christ, he is under discipline. It is by this obedience that he learns the meaning of his calling to be a Christian. From this need for discipline come the phrases "rule of life" and "imitation of Christ."

In I Peter, written to Christians under persecution, the reader learns what it means to be like Jesus. The Christian imitates him in his obedience to the Father's purposes; he is steadfast in the face of suffering; he witnesses for the faith courageously, yet often in silence. This is the ultimate test of discipleship: the willingness to share in Christ's sufferings. But the suffering of the Christian is not in order to save the world. Its purpose is to point to the Christian's Lord, whose own death and resurrection have been for the salvation of mankind. So the Christian witness points to God's work and his purpose.

Christian discipline means a life lived in the world and yet apart from the world. How can that be? Because he lives in the presence of God and knows himself to be part of a company, the church, belonging to God in a special way. He has been set apart by his Baptism. First-century Christians were known for their kindness, not only to their own people, but to anyone in need of help. This was an unusual degree of concern. When non-Christians asked, "Why do you help us?" they replied that they were simply trying to show to others the love of God already made known to them.

It would have been easier, in a way, to try to practice the love of God only among their own group, but then no one else would ever have known about it. On Sundays, in their worship together, they could strengthen one another. At other times theirs was the more difficult task of going about everyday tasks in a new spirit. This is still the discipline of the Christian life: to be persons through whom God's Holy Spirit can shine forth to all people, even when those to whom the Christian goes do not comprehend; indeed, even when they misunderstand, distort, or deliberately cause those to suffer who persist in acting as followers of Christ.

See OBEDIENCE.

DOCTRINE "Doctrine" and "dogma" both have the same basic meaning: "a teaching." Doctrine is the intellectual content of the Christian faith, the teaching that can be put into words.

The Christian faith begins with a proclamation of the good news of how God offers salvation to all people through Christ. This message is explained in several forms of teaching. The creed, or affirmation of faith, is a simple form that the believer affirms at his Baptism. This is a briefly stated formulation of what the Christian believes about God and his work. It contains Christian doctrine in its simplest form. (See CREED.)

The definition of doctrine began soon after the church emerged from widespread persecution and was accepted within the Roman Empire. The Council of Nicaea formulated in 325 A.D. the first such statement of faith. It was especially concerned to express the Christian understanding of the nature of Christ. Other councils followed in the course of centuries. The mainstream branches of the Christian church regard the decisions of these councils as more or less binding, depending on their particular understandings. Some Protestant groups do not recognize church council decisions as acceptable sources for doctrine, believing that all teaching (doctrine) is to be found in the Bible and that interpretation lies with the believer, taught by the Holy Spirit.

Doctrine (or dogma) is an attempt to put teaching into

specific words so that a person will have a reason for the faith that he holds. In this way he can explain to himself, or to others who ask. He can explain to those who are interested in knowing what a Christian believes, or who are seeking instruction because they believe. There will always be variations in the interpretation of doctrine. Some basic formulations are necessary so that there is a recognized unity for the presentation of Christianity to those of other beliefs as well as for those within the widespread areas of the Christian church itself.

E

EASTER   Easter is the high holy day of the Christian year. It is the foremost feast and was probably the first special day to be celebrated in the Christian calendar. Easter is the celebration of the resurrection, the remembrance of the day on which Jesus Christ rose from the dead.

Easter is the one holy day in the Christian year that is derived from the ancient reckoning of holidays by the moon, for Easter is calculated from the Passover season, which comes at the beginning of spring. Specifically, Easter occurs on the first Sunday after the first full moon after the vernal equinox (which is March 21, the first day of spring). That is why it is sometimes celebrated in March and sometimes in April. Since the crucifixion is supposed to have occured on a Friday and the resurrection on the third day following, "the first day of the week," it always occurs on a Sunday. Indeed, the Christian practice of having worship on Sunday rather than on the Sabbath, when as Jews they had been accustomed to gathering for worship, stems from this fact. Sunday is the weekly celebration of the resurrection.

Although the English name for the day comes from that of an ancient Germanic goddess of spring, the word in most other languages recalls the fact that this is the Paschal (Passover) Feast. Judaism celebrates the deliverance from

Egyptian slavery by eating the Passover lamb. Christians, calling Christ the Lamb of God sacrificed for men, celebrate his victory over sin and death.

Easter is not simply a day, but a season. It is forty days long and covers the time that the Gospels have assigned as the period during which the risen Lord appeared at various times to his disciples. So the Easter season is a time for recalling all the Easter narratives—of his appearance at the tomb, on the Emmaus road, in an upper room, by the Sea of Galilee, and finally on the Mount of Olives outside Jerusalem. Easter stretches from Resurrection Day to Ascension Day. So the church continues to celebrate the day in the continued use of the Easter hymns and the reading of these passages from the Gospels. The color for the season is white, for it is a time of rejoicing.

See LENT; RESURRECTION.

ELECT, THE   Everyone knows what an election is. It is a time when people choose from among their number those to whom they wish to entrust certain public offices. No matter how much a person may desire a particular office, he cannot, under this system, have it by his own efforts. He may have certain abilities and he can try to persuade the voters, but the power to elect lies outside himself.

The Bible also speaks about election. The people of Israel were elected—chosen by God to be his own special people. They were a people of the covenant, the agreement by which God chose them to be his people and promised that as they were faithful he would always be their God, guiding and strengthening them. It became apparent through the centuries that their election did not guarantee them power or success, but often brought only suffering. They were elected to show by their very existence that their God was the living God, the creator of mankind and the ruler of his world.

The Christian is also a person elected by God. God sent Jesus into the world to show his love. Jesus chose the Twelve —they did not merely decide that they wanted to follow him. However, although they were not free to make themselves disciples, they were free to refuse to become disciples had they wanted to. In fact, Judas finally betrayed him and, choosing death, gave up his discipleship. Peter, on the other hand, denied him, but quickly turned in remorse, was forgiven and restored to the group.

After Jesus' appearances among his disciples had ceased, he sent his Holy Spirit into their midst as they went out to preach the good news and to call others to be his followers. The Acts of the Apostles records that "the Lord added to their number day by day those who were being saved" (Acts 2:47).

The Christian church knows this still to be true. One does not join the church as he does a club, because of what it will do for him. Whether he realizes it or not, one joins the church because God has first called him. People resist that call, even for years. They may, if they wish, resist it for a lifetime. But if they respond to his love and are obedient to his call, they become part of a fellowship of believers that extends around the world and has been in existence for nearly two thousand years.

The Christian is elected to eternal life, for he belongs to God. God has saved the whole world in Christ, but the gift of his salvation is not forced upon anyone. It is given to those who willingly accept their election.

The Christian is chosen in order that he may witness to what God has done and show others that they are called. Sometimes this witness involves suffering and even death. It may require a radical change in the way of life. But the Christian never suffers alone. He is upheld by the grace of God and sustained by the fellowship of other Christians.

Theologians have debated as to whether God elects everyone. The Bible says that in Christ, God reconciled the world unto himself. Then the questions arise: Since God is all-powerful, can anyone refuse his call? Since he is loving, would he let anyone refuse salvation? Love always involves suffering, and the love of God opens even the Holy One to the possibility of suffering. This is the meaning of the cruci-fixion—the suffering of God. Only if men are free, can they respond to God's love, for no one (even God) can force another person to love him. Through the beauty of the world, through the love of Christ, through the affections of human beings, God seeks to persuade people to accept their election as his own. But the response must be freely given.

EPIPHANY Epiphany was celebrated in the Christian church before a date was set for Christmas. The word means "an appearance" and usually refers to a divine appearance. So Epiphany celebrates the fact that God appeared among men in human form in the person of his Son. The date is January 6. It is the holy day in which the coming of Christ is remembered.

Later, when Christmas became celebrated as the day of the birth of Jesus in Bethlehem, Epiphany took on a special meaning as the celebration of the appearance of God in Christ to the Gentiles (those who did not belong to Israel). The story of the Wise Men became associated with this day, for they were popularly supposed to have come from distant lands, following a star, seeking the promised One.

The Epiphany season, in the calendar of the Christian year, lasts for as many as six weeks. Since the length of the season has to be figured backward from the date of Easter in any given year, through the forty days of Lent, and three Sundays in pre-Lent, the length of the Epiphany season will vary. The color is white during the octave (eight days from January 6 to 13) and green thereafter. Traditionally, the Gospel readings for these Sundays record the various events in which Jesus seemed to be showing forth his divinity: as a child in the Temple, in the appearance of the dove at his baptism, at the marriage in Cana, in the healing of the lepers, and at the time of judgment.

During this season which follows Christmas, the church reminds itself that Jesus is the Christ, the Son of the living God, and that he was sent among men to show what God is like. The emphasis is on the glory of his appearing. Thus Christians, knowing their own faith, can proclaim him among men, even as the Wise Men returned to their own people to tell the wondrous things that they had seen.

See ADVENT; CHRISTMAS.

EPISTLE An epistle is a letter. The New Testament contains a number of letters, some written to churches, a few to individuals. Most of these letters were written by the apostle Paul to the churches that he had started. One was written to a church in Rome that he planned to visit. Sometimes a letter was sent because of a problem that was troubling the church. Indeed, in writing to Corinth, he said that if they did not settle the problem, he would come himself, and he did. Later, he wrote a gentle letter, assuring them of his love and concern for them. Sometimes the letter was written to explain the meaning of the Christian faith. Galatians, for example, has been called "the charter of Christian freedom," for in it Paul explains that to him real freedom can be known only in freely willed surrender and obedience to Christ.

Some letters were written to individuals: I and II Timothy, Titus, and Philemon, for example. The letter to Philemon is as brief as a personal letter today might be. Paul is sending back to Philemon a slave who had run away but who had since become a Christian. He commends the slave, Onesimus, to his master as a brother in Christ. Some letters were written to be read in a number of congregations. First Peter was addressed to groups under persecution. The opening chapters of The Revelation to John are addressed to the churches in the province of Asia, and there is a specific message for each of seven churches. Letters usually include advice as to how the Christian ought to act as he lives in a non-Christian world.

A letter usually opens with a greeting, develops the matters at hand, and often ends with specific messages to individuals and families known to the writer and a final blessing.

There is a personal quality about these letters that makes the churches seem alive. However, the subject matter of the letters often seems complicated and requires an understanding of the background through some serious study. Most of them are brief, but not easy reading. The beginner would do well to start with Philemon and Philippians.

ETERNAL LIFE   Eternal life is the gift of God to those who will accept it. The understanding is summed up in John 17:3: "This is eternal life, that they know thee the only true God, and Jesus Christ whom thou hast sent." Eternal life, then, is the "knowledge" of God through Christ.

"Know" is a word of deep meaning. To know a person involves not only knowing *about* him but an understanding *of* him. The word "knowing" involves relationship.

The Bible assumes that God knows us because he has created us and we belong to him. But how can man know God? He can do this only as God makes himself known. The Christian finds God made known most clearly in the person of Jesus Christ, crucified and risen. (See REVELATION.)

To know God means to recognize that, as a human being, one is sinful. Only God can forgive the sin and make possible a new relationship with him in the gift of his Holy Spirit. Those who live by the power of his Spirit have eternal life now. This does not mean that they will never sin, but only that God will continue to help them to be more faithful in their obedience to him. When they fall, he will raise them up. So they will never die, for they will never be completely absent from him or be left without the power of his love. Baptism is the sign and seal of this new life in Christ. (See BAPTISM.)

This work, begun in the earthly life of the Christian, knows no break in the death of the body. The apostle Paul says that this physical body is raised a spiritual body. (I Cor. 15:44.) Eternal life is a continuing life, a quality of life, a state of existence.

There is always a sense of mystery in the Christian's understanding of eternal life. He knows the nature of its present form, but he does not know its form after death. He is given confidence in two ways. He has the remembrance of the first disciples who saw their risen Lord. The death of the body that could not hold him would not hold them either. They kept many stories of his appearances to them and these have been given to us through the records in the Gospels. Moreover, in his present life, he knows that God in whom he believes and whom he serves is constantly saving, supporting, helping, and loving him. Thus he feels assured that God will not fail him in death. This is the faith which has kept Christians serene in crises and helped them to endure suffering courageously.

The Revelation to John is a symbolic writing, describing the terrors of a church under persecution. But it ends with the picture of a city not made with hands where God shall be the light and the comfort of his people. In the Fourth Gospel, just before his betrayal Jesus speaks to his disciples and assures them that he goes to prepare a place for them so that where he is there they may be also. He adds that he will come and take them to himself. (John 14:2–3.) Such passages have always been guideposts to Christians, illuminating the mystery. They have not asked to see clearly, for they have trusted him who is their guide.

See DEATH.

EVANGELISM Evangelism is the telling of the good news of Jesus Christ to the whole world. The word "evangelism" comes from the Greek word *euangelion,* which means "glad tidings."

The Christian church has always had good news to tell to the whole world. The first Christians were people who heard the apostles tell the story of Jesus. They were sure that in this person, who loved and healed, died and rose from the dead, God had come among men in a special way to draw them to himself. As each in turn saw that God is love, as each knew repentance and began a new way of life, he realized that he had been turned around—converted. His relationship to God was a new one; so was his relationship to other people. He felt release and joy. Whether a slave or a nobleman, his life was different. The people among whom he lived noticed the difference. Indeed, one ancient writer notes that the people said in amazement, "See how these Christians love one another." It was also said that Christians were turning the world upside down.

Love and joy are not feelings that a person keeps to himself. They are meant to be shared with others. So Christians have always shared with others the love that God had shown to them and the joy with which he had filled their lives. Jesus had commanded his disciples to go into the whole world and preach the gospel (good news). They gladly obeyed this command.

The motive for evangelism is this: that those who have not known Christ may know him. It has sent Christian missionaries into every part of the world. Christian congregations have been started in every continent. Schools have been built in far corners of the earth to teach people to read, enabling them to read for themselves the words of the good news in the Bible. Missionaries have translated the Bible or parts of it into almost every language known to men. They have established hospitals to heal (remembering that Jesus healed) and to show that the power of God is extended to men in love and goodness, never to harm or make them fearful.

The good news has been preached in every corner of the earth. Yet many have not heard it and many who have heard have not responded. Even in countries where Christianity is almost the only religion, there are people who have not really heard it. They have lived in an atmosphere in which no one speaks of God and in which people, sometimes very good people, have thought that there is no God and that man must show love and courage because he is human. They cannot "prove" God the way they can prove a scientific fact, and so they do not believe that God cares about them.

The good news is addressed to them also. Not many people can feel self-sufficient all the time. But they can only respond to the good news at the point where their own resources have failed them. When all goes well, people do not think they need God. Only in their weakness are they open to his saving love.

Jesus knew this when he said that the poor, the meek, the mourners, the pure in heart, were blessed. (See BEATITUDES.) They are the ones who can hear the good news and be turned by it. To those who are able to receive, God gives his Spirit; these he receives into his Kingdom.

See CONVERSION; GOSPEL, THE.

EVIL   Evil is a power in the world that works against God's good purposes. Sometimes evil results from the deliberate purposes of men; at other times evil seems to be beyond man's power either to prevent or to overcome. This power has been named the devil, Satan, or the evil one. (See SATAN.) It is real; it is subject to the final purposes of God.

Some people are puzzled as to how evil can exist if God is good. They have reasoned that perhaps God is not all-powerful. The Christian faith has rejected this possibility. The Bible pictures God as giving human beings the freedom to choose good or evil. They may choose to serve him, in which case he will guide and strengthen them, even in times of suffering and evil. Or they may choose to live for themselves, in which case they will come into the power of evil, which will distort and destroy their true lives. By having to choose between good and evil, they have the possibility of rejecting God instead of responding to him. Freedom, which is the gift of God, makes it possible for man to do evil.

Why does God permit this to happen? He places this self-limitation upon himself because he loves mankind. He seeks by every means to win men's love, but he cannot force it. No one can force another person to love him. God can forgive and receive again those who turn from evil to serve him. There is a mystery to evil that can only be accepted.

God's triumph over evil is shown in the gospel story. Jesus came bringing God's love in word and deed. But evil forces working in men and in their whole society caused his death. These men thought that they were doing good, that they were saving their nation and their religion. To the disciples, however, it seemed as if evil had triumphed and God's good purpose had been defeated. Easter Day changed all this. In raising Jesus from the dead, God showed that his power was greater than all the power of evil. The triumph of righteousness had begun. It would not be completed until the end of the world, but there were signs.

Evil exists in the world because God permits it. He created a good world in which joy and love can exist. He rules his world and can limit the power of the evil forces that operate in the world. Moreover, he is with his people when they are overwhelmed by evil, either individually or collectively. His faithfulness is their comfort and assurance.

Sometimes evil directly serves the good purposes of God. It strengthens people in good purposes. It makes vivid the need for change. The good can become more desirable when seen alongside evil. But the Christian is never content to permit evil to exist. This is the center of the struggle: that evil, which in Christ's victory has been overcome by example, may in God's time and with his help be vanquished from all human existence. This, ultimately, is the work of God.

See SIN.

F

FAITH The classical definition of faith is to be found in Heb. 11:1 and it is followed by examples of the men of faith throughout Biblical history. They trusted God when they could not see ahead or understand what he was calling them to do.

Faith must not be confused with belief. Faith precedes belief. One can speak of a *"belief about"* and having *"faith in.*" Belief is the formulation in words of what faith is. In some languages there is a verb something like "I faith," but in present-day English the nearest equivalent is "I believe in."

Faith is near to trust. When a person has faith in someone, it means he puts himself in that person's hands. Usually, a person trusts only someone whom he loves, as a child trusts his parents to do for him what is best. A person also trusts someone of whose ability he is sure. When one rides in an airplane, a boat, or a train, one's life is entrusted to the pilot, the captain, or the engineer. One tends to put trust in a person only when one feels unable to handle a situation oneself.

Someone has compared faith in God to being in deep water. When a person knows that he cannot hold himself up, he turns to God, who holds, supports, and sustains him. This happens only when one lets the initiative belong to God. The person who struggles goes down.

This is not "blind faith," which would be trusting in that which one does not know. There are times when one has to go through a situation blindly, and hoping for the best. But the Christian knows the God in whom he puts his faith. He reads of what God has done for his people in the Bible; he sees God in Jesus and knows what God has done for others. He is thus able to be sure that God can free him from sin, fill him with love, sustain him in suffering, and help him to overcome evil.

However, the impulse of the human being is to do everything for himself. He distrusts rather than trusts. He feels safest when he is taking care of himself. To have faith, then, is somehow contrary to human nature. Therefore, faith is a gift of God. When God's love is recognized, it leads people to respond in faith. The Bible sometimes uses the phrase "their eyes were opened and they believed." God has been acting for them even when they thought the work was their own. When they were able to see the action of God in events, faith became possible. Jesus said once to his disciples that if they had faith as a grain of mustard seed (which is very tiny) they would be able to move mountains. (Matt. 17:20.) That is a powerful picture. He meant that God could work with even the smallest response of faith and by his Holy Spirit increase it. To God, all things are possible, and in the power that comes from God, his people have been able to endure persecution, overcome obstacles, preach the good news everywhere in the world, and so live that nonbelievers were turned to him. This living faith in the saving work of God has sustained the church and has assisted each individual Christian triumphantly through every time of need.

FALL The understanding of the Fall is an interpretation that Christian theology has made of the story in Gen., ch. 3. There it tells how Adam and Eve dwelt in the Garden of Eden in which God had placed them; how Eve was tempted by the serpent to eat fruit from the tree of the knowledge of good and of evil, which God had forbidden them to touch; how she persuaded Adam to join her; and what God did about it when he found out, expelling them from the garden to live a more difficult life outside.

This narrative is understood as myth, that is, a story in which universal terms are used to explain a truth and to answer a basic question about life. Men have always asked the questions: How did evil come into the world? and Why is there so much pain and suffering? The story of Adam and Eve tries to give answers. The word "Adam" means "man" or "human being." Adam represents all members of the human race. God offers to his human children a world that he has created to be good. But human beings are constantly distorting this goodness by their self-centeredness, their assurance that they can get along without God, and their determination to make the world what they will instead of what God wills. The writer of the story assumes that once people were innocent, knowing only the good. The dangerous gift, which was to know good and evil, was taken without God's permission. This necessitated choice, and the choice between good and evil has been a basic part of human life.

Biblical history, and history since then, seems to indicate that given free choice, man often chooses evil and destruction, and that only by loving God and seeking his purposes can he choose good.

This is the Fall: that human beings love God only partly, and so choose disobedience, which is sin, rather than faithfulness, which is eternal life. Man's problem is not that he is human but that he is sinful. He finds life fulfillment in dominating others rather than in serving God.

See ORIGINAL SIN.

FAMILY   The Bible speaks of "the Father, from whom every family in heaven and on earth is named" (Eph. 3:14) and by so doing broadens the understanding of the word "family." The modern family is thought of as consisting primarily of parents and children (sometimes grandparents), but it also includes related aunts, uncles, and cousins. The Old Testament family was so large that it constituted a tribe, each made up of smaller family units. The oldest member of the family was the leader, and his word was law. All the family prospered together, and all the family suffered together. No individual could act on his own responsibility. If one member of a tribe broke a serious law, the whole family was punished.

Similarly in the New Testament, when one member of a family responded to the gospel, the whole family became a part of the Christian community. It is said of Paul's jailer that he was baptized with his whole family. (Acts 16:33.)

When the Bible uses the word "father," it is referring to one who is the center of the family, as well as its ruler. The welfare of the family depends upon him. The son is one who honors, obeys, and loves the father and receives strength through him. As the commandment indicates (Ex. 20:12), fathers and mothers are both to be honored by their children.

The New Testament broadens the understanding of "children" beyond that of the family. The writers spoke of one another as "children" of God, for they believed that through

Christ they had been made sons of God. They thought of themselves as brothers to one another, having a mutual responsibility in love.

The family is part of God's creation. He placed families in the world to enjoy it and to serve him. Families in various forms exist everywhere on earth, regardless of the religion that they practice.

The Christian family is one in which the members know themselves to be redeemed by Christ. They are a part of God's new covenant by their Baptism, and thus a part of his church. This is why parents want their children to receive Baptism, make their confession of faith, have religious education, and join in the worship of the church. The New Testament has several things to say about how Christians act in families, but primarily their love for one another, and toward others, is an example to the world.

FASTING Fasting is a Biblical custom that probably meant going without food for a stated length of time. It was used in times of mourning, as a sign of repentance, or to reinforce a petition. The priests in the Old Testament fasted before making certain sacrifices. Families fasted at a time of death. The whole people fasted at times of national calamity: when drought threatened the harvest or they were defeated in war. These disasters seemed to be the punishment of God for sin. Fasting was a solemn time when the people could reexamine their deeds and ask forgiveness.

Those who fasted were reminded that their lives were filled with goodness which came only from God. It brought the realization that they were dependent upon him.

In the time of Jesus, fasting twice a week was regularly a part of Jewish religion. The disciples of John the Baptist fasted, but Jesus and his disciples did not. He explained that his presence was a time of rejoicing and not a time for fasting. The practice reappeared in the early church. They fasted on special occasions when serious decisions were made (Acts 13:2; 14:23). Fasting was never to be done for self-improvement, for only God could enable a person to grow in grace and goodness. But the Christian life was likened by Paul to that of an athlete in training (I Cor. 9:24 f.), and one could take whatever discipline was necessary for the gospel's sake.

Eventually the custom arose of a Friday fast in weekly remembrance of the crucifixion. Today even in Christian groups that note fast dates on the calendar, the "fast" seldom consists of more than eating fish instead of meat. The Lenten fast, which has varied in length of time, as now practiced is forty days long, not including Sundays. It extends from Ash Wednesday to the day before Easter. Around it has often grown the practice of "giving up" habits, practices, or luxury foods as a form of "discipline." This is supposed in some way to be a reminder of the sacrifice of Christ and to prepare the Christian for the joy of Easter. As such, it needs serious rethinking. In fact, the whole place of fasting in religious practice needs to be reexamined.

FEAR   "Fear" is a word whose basic meaning everyone understands, even without definition. To fear a person or a thing is to avoid or shrink from that person or thing. It is the opposite of trust and of love. The Bible speaks of fearing one's enemies. Sometimes the enemies are an invading nation; sometimes they are enemies of the spirit—envy, pride, and so on.

God is the one who can deliver a person from fear and remove the object feared. The form in which the psalmist usually voices a prayer for the release from fear is that God will remove the enemy, and he will not have to be afraid. But what if God does not? Then the prayer can only be for power to withstand the enemy and for eventual deliverance. This release from fear is part of the good news that the New Testament tells. Jesus prayed in the Garden to be spared, but his deliverance came after the crucifixion. To meet and vanquish the enemy in the power of the Holy Spirit has been part of the Christian's warfare.

The Bible also uses the phrase "the fear of God." This

does not mean that people should be afraid of God. The word usually means "awe." It is a realization of the vast difference between God, the Creator, the Holy One, on whom all life depends, and his human children. However close the relationship between God and man, man must recognize this difference. It has been bridged by the love of God, but God's love is different from human love, for he remains faithful in spite of human indifference, disobedience, and rejection. The fear (awe) of God is expressed in the psalmist's words, sometimes translated: "O worship the Lord in the beauty of holiness; let the whole earth stand in awe of him" (Ps. 96:9, *The Book of Common Prayer*).

FELLOWSHIP   Fellowship is a word that is often used in the Bible. It does not always carry some of the meanings that we give to it. Fellowship does not mean a gathering of people who like one another, in order to have a good time together. As a theological word "fellowship" has a much deeper meaning.

Fellowship is used in the Old Testament to refer to associations among *people*, a group joined together in common work. It is never used with reference to a common relationship to God, for that would seem to indicate too much familiarity for human beings to have with the holy One.

Fellowship is used in the New Testament to refer to the relationship that Christians have with Christ. It speaks of sharing in Christ or with Christ: to live with Christ, to suffer with Christ, and so on. It speaks also of fellowship with the Father, for God has come to men in Jesus Christ and it is no longer an irreverence to use the phrase. This is a vertical form of fellowship: between men and their Redeemer.

Christians also knew a bond of fellowship with one another, a horizontal one. This fellowship lies in the fact that each person has been called by God to be a member in Christ. They have not chosen one another; God has brought them together in the church. They belong to one another because they belong to Christ and are trying to live faithfully for him. This bond of fellowship lies in the action of the Holy Spirit, who indwells each one and so indwells the church, making it a divine fellowship.

Christians are enabled to live by their faith daily because they know that others are also trying to live in obedience to Christ. This makes it possible for them to stand up for their faith when people are unfriendly and even to witness for Christ when they might have to suffer by doing so. They know that others are encouraging them, praying for them, and are willing to share in their suffering.

This fellowship enables Christians to have friends even when they are a small group living in a non-Christian country. Their faith becomes more important to them then. They feel a special responsibility for living as Christians in order to show others the nature of the Christian faith and the quality of the love of God as expressed through them.

The fellowship within the church is not perfect, for Christians are human and the work of the Holy Spirit does not make them otherwise. Even in the first years of the church, the apostle Paul had to write to the church at Corinth telling them to settle a quarrel in their midst. But if the bonds of fellowship could be broken, they could also be restored. Because of their common love for Christ, Christians can find in their worship together the means of healing their differences. This is a divine fellowship made up of human beings. Their love is imperfect; their lives are imperfect—but in times of crisis they can do great things for God. Their works of service for those outside the church—feeding the hungry, healing the sick, helping the oppressed, teaching and preaching—have formed their witness to what God intended the fellowship of the church to be.

So when the word "fellowship" is used to describe the church, it ought to mean the community of those who meet together for worship and who go forth into their everyday lives to bear witness through their work in the world.

FESTIVAL A festival is a feast day, a day of rejoicing and thanksgiving. It is a day or a series of days for joyous remembrance of an event through which God has helped and saved his people. The Old Testament describes a number of festivals. Some of these surround the creative work of God in the planting and the harvest. Others are connected with God's saving work. The Passover season comes in the spring, and during this time the people recall how God brought them out of Egypt, saw them safely across the Red Sea where they thought they would be destroyed, and set them on the way toward their Promised Land. Later there is Pentecost, a re-calling of God's gift of the Law. In the autumn, there is the solemn Day of Atonement, when they remember before God their sins and his forgiveness; the beginning of the new year, and the Feast of Booths, a harvest festival in which they remember how God cared for them during their wan-derings when they had no real home. Two festivals come from later Jewish history: Purim, in the spring, which recalls the story of Esther; and the Feast of Lights, in December, which recalls how Judas Maccabaeus and his family with-stood the pagan Greeks.

The Christian calendar is built around New Testament events. It begins with the preparation for the birth of Christ, continues by recalling how he showed in his life the nature of God, reaches a climax in the events of Holy Week and the Easter season, and goes from Pentecost, celebrating the gift of the Holy Spirit to the church, into the half year of the Trinity season, the celebration of God the Creator. In the spring it parallels the Jewish calendar. The events surround-ing the death of Christ were set in the context of the Pass-over (his followers thought of him as the Lamb of God taking away the sins of the world). The Christian Pentecost, celebrating the gift of the Holy Spirit, parallels the Jewish emphasis in that season on the gift of the Law.

See CHURCH YEAR.

FORGIVENESS Three different Hebrew words are used in the Old Testament to describe forgiveness. These are words which mean "to cover up," "to carry away," and "to let go." When one is forgiven, there is no longer any barrier or resentment. The broken relationship is restored. The Greek words used in the New Testament for forgiveness have similar meanings: they suggest "to be gracious to," and "send away."

The pardon of God is always dependent upon the repentance of man. Sin cannot be forgiven until there is a turning around, a change of mind and of intention. Only when the person desires to live differently can his sin be forgiven. In the Old Testament, when a person brings a sin offering to the priest in the Temple, it is not meant to pay for his sin but only to be a symbol of the fact that he will try to make amends for his wrongdoing. God expected those seeking forgiveness to show repentance.

Forgiveness is sought because wrongdoing brings a sense of guilt that is a real burden. People cannot live this way long. It oppresses them. They know that something is wrong, both in their relationships to other people and in their relationship to God. Forgiveness is necessary to any human happiness. This is why the forgiveness of sin is looked upon as a release.

In the Bible there is no limit to the forgiveness of God. The phrase "seventy times seven" (Jesus' answer to the disciple who asked how often one should forgive) is simply a phrase meaning that it is useless to count how often one should forgive. (See Matt. 18:22.) So also is the forgiveness of God: there is no limit upon it, just as there is no limit to the grace of God, his outgoing love. The phrase of the apostle Paul that links forgiveness with "being gracious to" a person is an understanding of the nature of God's forgiveness. It brings about a situation in which the grace of God can again flow through a human life, enabling him to live faithfully and obediently.

There is one requirement for any one hoping to receive this forgiveness: the willingness to forgive others. There is a parable in which Jesus tells of a man who would not forgive another person a small debt, and who was condemned by his master to be punished for his own enormous debt.

(Matt. 18:23–35.) The Lord's Prayer says, "Forgive us our debts, as we forgive our debtors." This is essential to the Biblical understanding of forgiveness. It might even be said that the one who is unable to forgive fellow beings is unable to repent of his sin, and is therefore shut off from receiving the forgiveness of God. This is the only sense in which sin can be unforgivable. A person can so live as to deaden himself to the possibility either of showing mercy to others or of being sorry for that which he himself does. Such a person is truly lost, for he has put himself beyond the possibility of the divine forgiveness, insofar as human beings seem able to understand forgiveness.

It is well to remember that forgiveness is something that comes from God. He extends his grace to his people and restores them to a new relationship with himself. Man can respond to what God offers, but he cannot offer anything to God first. So repentance and forgiveness are gifts of God by which God shows his love to his children.

See SIN.

FREEDOM Human freedom is a gift of God, according to the Bible. It is contained in man's free choice to do good or evil; he can live in fulfillment of God's purposes or seek only the fulfillment of his own purposes.

Freedom is necessary for love. If God were simply an absolute and impersonal ruler, this would not matter. He could even manipulate his creatures for their own good and easily make the world perfect. But in the Bible the nature of God is love; he wants creatures who can respond to his love. This can happen only as there is freedom for the growth of a relationship of love. God invites man, but man may accept or reject God. This is the nature of the decision that must be made.

Some think freedom means that a person can do whatever he wishes. That would not be freedom but license. No one is free who does whatever he wants; he is a slave to his wants. No one is free who hurts another person by his actions; such a one is bound by his own egotism. The apostle Paul writes that he is a slave of Christ, and that in this obedience is found perfect freedom. It does not seem possible that slavery can be freedom, but this was his experience. Before belonging to Christ, he was always anxious as to whether he was doing right or wrong; he was even bound by his own desire to be good. When he responded to the love of God and knew that his life was guided by the Holy Spirit, the anxiety left. By seeking only to obey Christ, his Lord, and to be a faithful apostle, he was freed from some decisions and guided in others. So he was able to write to one of the churches that a man who thought himself free was often a slave, but that a follower of Christ, even though he might legally be a slave, had an inner freedom. The Christian is free because Christ has freed him from the power of sin. The release from the power of sin and freedom for the perfect service of God, however, is a continuous growth through the work of the Holy Spirit. This inner freedom is, in Christian thought, the only true freedom.

G

GLORY Because the reality of God is so deeply wonderful and because he is so great and all-powerful, religious people have always used imaginative terms in which to describe him as he shows himself in his creation.

The Bible is filled with references to "the glory of God." In the Old Testament we read of the way in which the Ark of the Covenant led the people of Israel in their desert wanderings as they sought the Promised Land. Exodus 13:21 ff. speaks of the pillar of smoke by day and the pillar of fire by night, which guided them. God's presence is made known by the "shekinah," the Hebrew term for his glorious appearance. The thorn bush from which Moses heard God's voice is an example of shekinah, or the countenance of Moses when he descended from Mt. Sinai, where he had seen the brightness of God's glory. Ezekiel in his writings describes the vision of God that came to him as his call to be a prophet, and he says, "Such was the appearance of the likeness of the glory of the Lord" (Ezek. 1:28). As years went on, people looked forward to a future time, at the coming of the Messiah, when God's glory would fill the earth.

In the New Testament the glory of God is attributed also to Jesus Christ. The glorious God comes to earth to make himself known in Jesus. The shepherds see this glory when they visit the Christ-child after his birth. It is shown at his baptism and at the transfiguration. In his death on the cross and in his resurrection, Jesus shows forth the glorious victory of God. As Paul wrote in II Cor. 4:6, "For it is the God who said, 'Let light shine out of darkness,' who has shone in our hearts to give the light of the knowledge of the glory of God in the face of Christ."

GOD One of the chief characteristics of man from the beginning of recorded history is his concern with ultimate questions. He asks why there is life on earth and what its meaning is. This is as true of primitive peoples as it is of highly civilized ones. It is impossible to find any group of people among whom such questions have not been asked.

Various answers have been given, according to the situation of the people involved. In almost every case, the explanations of the meaning of life are based on the sense of a reality that is greater than man himself. Alone, faced by the vast spaces of the heavens, the mystery of nature, the broad oceans, the occurrence of birth and death, man does not feel secure in the world that he inhabits. He reaches for answers to his Why? and senses in the world a mysterious presence. He reaches out for a Power greater than himself who can give his life meaning and afford him protection. In other words, he needs God to give his life wholeness and completeness.

Many explanations have been given for the idea of God. Some believe that men worship God out of a sense of dependence and need. Others have believed that such worship is due to a sense of the mystery of existence. Others have insisted that the idea of God is really an illusion, that God is only a projection of man's own self.

The Jewish-Christian tradition rejects all these interpretations. The Biblical view does not talk about the "idea of God" but knows the reality of God himself, who is not an idea but a living Being. God makes himself known and calls to the persons whom he has created. The Bible assumes God to start with. He is not the result of man's efforts to explain a universe he does not fully understand. He is the active participant in the universe he himself has created and which he sustains by his almighty power. "In the beginning God created the heavens and the earth." (Gen. 1:1.) The whole record of the Bible is the story of how God reaches out to those who seek him. They understand who he is as they respond to him in faithful service and love. They can turn against him, in which case they may despair. Or they can say yes to him and receive blessedness and meaning in life as they fulfill the purposes for which he has created them. God makes himself known through historical happenings: in the deliverance of the Israelites from bondage in Egypt, in the warnings of prophets, and supremely in the life, death, and resurrection of Jesus Christ. The God of the Bible is not some far-off potentate of the skies who comes or shows himself peekaboo fashion. Nor is he like the gods of the pagans, who think they can persuade the gods to do what the worshipers want by means of sacrifices that are pleasing. Rather, he is one who is faithful to his own promises that he has made known. He wants his people to be faithful to him.

GOOD FRIDAY   The remembrance of Jesus' death on the cross became a part of the church's annual Lenten observances. By the early Middle Ages the day came to be marked by various special observances. It was regarded as a fast day on which only the most essential food should be eaten. The altars were stripped bare and the sacrament of the Holy Communion was not celebrated again until Easter Day. In the medieval church special dramatic exercises (miracle plays) were enacted in the churchyards by traveling troupes. They would depict the events of the crucifixion. Some of these developed into the Passion plays, which eventually covered all the events of Jesus' last week on earth and ended with the resurrection. (Oberammergau, Germany, is the home of one of the famous Passion cycles that have continued into modern times.)

Why is the Friday on which Jesus was crucified called "good"? It would seem to be anything but good, for an innocent man suffered death and his disciples were stricken with great fear. It was in the light of the resurrection that they could call it "good." What men intended for evil, God in his almighty power turned to good—the greatest good of all: the victory of light over darkness, truth over falsehood, love over hatred, life over death.

See CROSS.

GOODNESS It is rather difficult to say what is meant by "goodness," although many people use the word constantly. Religious people are said to be "good" people, although they would hesitate to apply the term to themselves. Usually it is interpreted rather negatively. "Goodness" means "not being bad." Here again some confusion appears. Does "being good" mean anything more than conforming to the standards of a social group? If one keeps all the customs of behavior expected in the circles within which he moves, such a person might be called good. But suppose the customs are themselves evil? History shows many examples of standards that under one set of circumstances were considered "correct" but which under changed circumstances had to be surrendered. Slavery has been abolished; crimes are less often punishable by death.

"Goodness" comes from the same root as "God." Once when

someone addressed him as "Good Teacher," Jesus said: "Why do you call me good? No one is good but God alone" (Mark 10:18). This statement of Jesus' indicates that only those can be said to be truly good who do not try hard to be so. The truly good person is one whose life is directed toward God, whom he seeks to serve not in order to receive rewards but for the honor of God himself. The term "pious" as it is often used implies the effort to seem good. True piety is goodness before God, purity of life, without worrying about the impression made on other people.

GOSPEL, THE The word "gospel" means "good news." The followers of Jesus had heard his preaching and teaching. They received his message that the reign of God was beginning in a new way on the earth. After Jesus' death and resurrection, his life, work, and teachings came to be seen as the good news itself. The good news was that God had sent a Savior to man, and they could receive God's gift of eternal life here and now by responding to Jesus in repentance and faith.

The Greek word for which "gospel" is a translation is *euangelion*. From that word comes also the word "evangelism." The early Christians recognized that theirs was a missionary task. They were to spread the good news of salvation to all who could be reached. The church has continued to do that down through the centuries. "Gospel" itself comes from the Anglo-Saxon *gōdspel*, which means "good story." The gospel, then, can be thought of simply as the story of how God has saved his people from their sins and given them new and complete life.

We can also use the term "gospel" to refer to the Christian faith as a whole. The Christian faith *is* the gospel. The church exists to proclaim the gospel and bring men into the fellowship of believers. The Christians' way of life is the living out of the gospel in word and deed. The sacraments are an acting out of the gospel. In Baptism, one is initiated into Christ's death and resurrection and made a member of his flock. In the Lord's Supper, believers are drawn into spiritual communion with the One who gives the gospel as they break bread together.

See REDEMPTION; SALVATION.

GRACE When an insurance premium is due, it is supposed to be paid on time. However, if for any reason the insured person who owes a premium forgets or is unable to pay the amount due, the insurance company usually will consider the policy to be in force even without payment for an additional thirty days known as a period of grace. This is nothing that the insured person owns or can demand: it is the freely offered goodwill of the company.

In theology, "grace" refers to the free, unmerited love of God that is offered to his children. There is nothing man can do to earn or demand his love. One cannot expect to get something from him by doing extra acts of kindness or charity, for example. God cannot be persuaded to do something against his will. But he loves and protects his own, even though they can never force or earn such love and protection.

In the Old Testament this gracious quality of God is usually referred to as "loving kindness," or "everlasting mercy." God wills peace and prosperity for his people. Even when they fail to keep the covenant, he withholds deserved punishment from them. However, at the Last Judgment all will be held accountable for their sins. The way in which they are to keep the covenant is to give strict obedience to the law of Moses. This is their expression of love and faithfulness.

The New Testament rejects the attempt at keeping the law as a way to fulfill God's requirements and assure blessedness. Paul wrote that he, like all men, was so incapable of pleasing God that even when he tried to do good in the most complete way he failed. "For I do not do the good I want, but the evil I do not want is what I do." (Rom. 7:19.) The gift of salvation to which the Law and the Prophets pointed has been fulfilled in Jesus Christ. All people are invited to receive the gift of God's grace by believing faith in Jesus Christ.

H

HEAVEN   The ancients thought of the universe as being three-storied. The earth was the center. Above were the heavens, associated with divinity; underneath, a dark mysterious realm, the abode of evil spirits. The way people thought about geography showed itself in their thoughts of where the spirits of the living went after death.

Actually, it was not until near the end of the time during which the Old Testament was written (that is, near the time of Jesus) that the Jewish people thought of individuals as having personal existence after death. The dead were thought to go to a sort of underworld, known as Sheol, where they stayed forevermore. They were not completely extinguished, but no longer possessed the individuality they had had on earth. The Jewish theologians of the period just before the New Testament, however, began to believe that life survived after death. They said that a just God would preserve all souls. The first Christians said that because God had raised Jesus from the dead, he would also give eternal life to those who knew the power of Jesus' resurrection.

In the course of time (remember the three-storied universe!) some theologians said that the righteous (the faithful in Christ) would have their spirits (or souls) kept in paradise. This is heaven, the abode of the righteous dead, where they will remain until the Last Judgment.

Few theologians put any great stress on the geographical location of heaven. In popular thinking there is a tendency to think of heaven as a place. Since God is everywhere in his world, it can safely be assumed that how and where the spirits of the dead reside is not a matter to worry about. God knows them and cares for them. They can never be lost from his presence. Paul refers to the dead as receiving a "spiritual body" that will supplant the physical body inhabited on earth. "The first man was from the earth, a man of dust; the second man is from heaven. As was the man of dust, so are those who are of the dust; and as is the man of heaven, so are those who are of heaven. Just as we have borne the image of the man of dust, we shall also bear the image of the man of heaven." (I Cor. 15:47–49.)

See DEATH; ETERNAL LIFE; HELL; PURGATORY.

HELL Just as the ancients, with their three-storied universe, tended to think of the divinity as belonging to the upper regions, so they associated the regions under the earth with evil spirits. It was thought that those who lived good lives while on earth would be rewarded in heaven. Those who had been evil on earth would receive punishment in the realm ruled by Satan.

The Jews, however, thought of the underworld region as Sheol, the abode of all the dead. Within that region there was one section in which the especially wicked would be gathered together. They called it Gehenna, named for the refuse dump outside Jerusalem.

In Christian thought, hell came to be associated with the realm controlled by Satan. The powers of evil that hold sway over people's lives can be broken only by the action of God. God has delivered men from death and the evil one by his love shown forth in Jesus Christ. All who respond to Christ are henceforth forevermore in his keeping. Those who say no to God will remain in the control of evil (Satan), and their destiny can only be hell. In this sense hell can be thought of not so much as a place as a state of separation from God.

Theologians of the church used to debate the question whether God chose some for eternal life(heaven) and others for eternal damnation (hell). Protests arose against the view that a loving God would choose to subject any of his children, no matter how evil, to everlasting punishment. It has been argued that even the worst of sinners will always be given another chance by God. The possibility remains, however, that some may so completely separate themselves by willful choice from the life-giving and life-sustaining Spirit of God that they do indeed become complete slaves to the powers of evil. Such may already experience hell while on earth, though they seem not to realize the fact. What happens to such totally evil persons after death is known only to God.

See DEATH; ETERNAL LIFE; HEAVEN; PURGATORY.

HERESY   When the Christian faith was young in the world, the followers of Jesus Christ lived in joyful awareness that God had done great things for them and the world through the one they acknowledged as Lord. Within a few years after Jesus' earthly ministry had ended, however, the members of the church began to reflect more deeply on the meaning of their faith. Then they began to look at their Christian experience and draw from it some basic understandings. These were expressed in the form of statements *about* their faith. Religion is the experience of faith; theology is the interpretation of the experience. Thus they began to be concerned with the beliefs they held in common. They were encouraged to do this by the fact that in conversation with one another they often shared ideas as to what their faith meant to them. In reaching out to win others to Christian faith they had to be able to state what the church really held to be true.

Also, there sometimes arose within the church difficult questions about doctrine. Various persons would hold different views. If the church was to be unified and strong, it would be necessary to iron out those differences and come to some agreement. For instance, it was necessary to decide about the relation of Jesus' humanity to his divinity. Some argued that Jesus was completely a heavenly being who had descended to earth and only seemed to be sharing in the common life of men. Others were interested in proving that Jesus was a man like other men, and said that he achieved divinity only because he completely obeyed God's will. In councils of the church, matters like these were debated, sometimes for many months or even years. In the matter just mentioned, the Council of Chalcedon went on record that Jesus was both true God and true man: his divinity and his humanity were combined in one person. As the Nicene Creed put it: "I believe . . . in one Lord Jesus Christ; . . . Very God of Very God; . . . being of one substance with the Father; . . . who for us men and our salvation came down from heaven, . . . and was made man." This became a confession of the commonly held faith of the church.

Anyone who departed from the beliefs agreed upon as essential for Christians was regarded as heretical. Church people always had considerable freedom to interpret according to their best understanding. However, any radical departure from accepted beliefs was regarded as dangerous to the unity of the church. Sometimes this caused disagreements, leading eventually to the formation of many separate church bodies. Sometimes the new church bodies that started on the basis of what was regarded at the time as heresy later became very rigid themselves, expelling heretics from *their* midst. Church history shows that sometimes heretics were cruelly treated, even executed, for their beliefs. More and more, Christians today agree that there are some basic doctrines on which there should be universal agreement. Within the whole church, though, there must be room for varieties of interpretation as long as these do not violate generally held convictions. It also seems to be agreed in the modern world that instead of burning heretics at the stake, the church should remember that God, rather than the church, is Judge when matters of conscience are involved.

See BELIEF; DOCTRINE.

HOLINESS   When something is referred to as "holy" this usually means that it is set apart as belonging to God. To use another word, it is "sacred." Thus we refer to the "Holy Scriptures" or to "Holy Communion," or sometimes to "holy" persons.

There is a deeper meaning in the word "holiness," however. It refers to the very nature and being of God himself.

Because God is so utterly beyond the limited powers of the human mind to grasp him in his fullness, he can only be thought of and approached with feelings of awe and wonder. Whenever man tries to contemplate the great and majestic One, he is made conscious of his weakness and sinfulness and at the same time drawn toward God by his perfect power and love.

This quality of God is more than perfect goodness, though that which is holy surely cannot be thought of as less than such. Nor is it a quality that can be achieved by any person on earth, no matter how close his relationship to God. Holiness belongs to God alone. It is sensed and recognized by those who come into his presence. They cannot possess this holiness, which belongs only to God, but they are cleansed and uplifted by it.

The awesomeness and purity of holiness are expressed in the sixth chapter of Isaiah. There the prophet describes his vision of the Lord. Heavenly beings in the presence of God called out, "Holy, holy, holy is the Lord of hosts; the whole earth is full of his glory" (Isa. 6:3). Isaiah writes that in the face of this vision he feels like "a man of unclean lips," dwelling "in the midst of a people of unclean lips; for my eyes have seen the King, the Lord of hosts" (v. 5). Thereupon a heavenly being takes a burning coal from the altar and touches his lips, saying, "Behold, this has touched your lips; your guilt is taken away, and your sin forgiven" (v. 7). By being in the presence of the holy One, Isaiah feels cleansed and strengthened. Now he is able to go forth to live in the world as one sent by God. He becomes God's messenger to the people. Anyone who truly comes into the presence of the holiness of God will become terribly aware of his human limitations. At the same time he will be lifted up by the same holiness.

Something of this understanding is brought out by Reginald Heber in his hymn:

Holy, Holy, Holy! Though the darkness hide thee,
Though the eye of sinful man thy glory may not see,

Only thou art holy; there is none beside thee
Perfect in power, in love, and purity.
See GOD.

HOLY SPIRIT Jesus promised his disciples that when he had left this earth he would return to them by sending the Holy Spirit. (See Acts 1:5, 8.)

The first Christians were convinced that he had indeed come back to them in the resurrection. Their reaction to his death had been one of dismay and loneliness. But the first Easter made them know that the risen Christ was with them, and would continue to be with his followers to the end of time.

Religious people had always believed that God could be known through the working of his mysterious Spirit in the lives of men. Among early peoples some individuals were thought to have special spiritual insight and power. Sometimes they had strange talents not possessed by ordinary persons. Among the Hebrews the prophets were thought to be specially commissioned for their work by the gift of God's Spirit, as in the case of Isaiah, Micah, and Ezekiel.

The Christians did not think of the Spirit of God apart from their understanding of God in the life and work of Jesus. The psalmist (Ps. 51:11) had written, "Cast me not away from thy presence, and take not thy holy Spirit from me." The Christians continued to pray thus. But they were sure that the Spirit who indeed came to guide them was the presence of the living Christ in their midst.

The Holy Spirit was not a gift to individuals but to the whole Christian community. At Pentecost the Christians knew themselves to be knit together into oneness by the presence of Christ in their midst, empowering them to go into the world to fulfill his commission to them.

One term used in the Bible for the Holy Spirit is "Comforter." Jesus promised that after he had left this earth God would send to his disciples the Comforter to guide them and lead them into all truth. (John 16:7; 14:16.) Christians have always been confident that no matter what happened to them they would be sustained by the power of God in Jesus Christ. This was especially important for the early Christians who faced persecution and suffering of various kinds. If they remained faithful to their Lord, they were able to endure these things with inner calm and peace.

The church can be thought of as the community of the Holy Spirit. To put it another way, the church is the Spirit-filled community. Whenever the church has forgotten its Lord, seeking power for power's sake or thinking of itself as an organization capable of doing good works through its own power, it has had little influence among men. Whenever it has thought of itself as the vehicle through which the Holy Spirit works to proclaim salvation to men and to heal the wounds of the world in the Spirit of Christ, it has brought glory to God and won many to faith.

It is important to note that the Holy Spirit is not referred to as "it." The Holy Spirit always is personal and is called "he," just as God and Jesus are. In speaking of the Holy Spirit, the reference is to God himself as he acts in his world.

See TRINITY.

HOPE   The Christian meaning of "hope" is difficult to understand because of the different way in which the word is used in ordinary speech. Usually "hoping" refers to a vague sort of future expectation. People hope for something they want very much to happen or that would be desirable as a solution to some problem they are facing. There is no assurance that things will turn out as they would like, but they have "high hopes."

Unlike that kind of hope, Christian hope is based on the assurance that comes from faith in God. The Christian, like everyone in the world, has problems and unsatisfied needs. He dreams of something better yet to come. But he bases his hope not on some future happening but on the fact that God has already given him the sure ground of hope in Jesus Christ.

The first Christians were dismayed and forlorn when Jesus was crucified. By the resurrection they knew that death had not killed him, but that his Spirit was going to be with them and all who believed in him to the end of time. This was the basis for their hope. As an epistle puts it: "Blessed be the God and Father of our Lord Jesus Christ! By his great mercy we have been born anew to a living hope through the resurrection of Jesus Christ from the dead." (I Peter 1:3.) Those words were written to Christians who were being persecuted by the Roman Government because they would not recognize the emperor as divine. Their "living hope" was based on the conviction of faith that all time and all events are in God's hands; in the Last Day his power would triumph. Even in the midst of difficulties they could hope that all men might share the joy that was in them despite their sufferings. As the passage in I Peter continues, "In this you rejoice, though now for a little while you may have to suffer various trials, so that the genuineness of your faith, more precious than gold which though perishable is tested by fire, may redound to praise and glory and honor at the revelation of Jesus Christ." (Ch. 1:6–7.)

The first Christians had such a "living hope" when they were a small, struggling, suffering minority in a pagan world. It is obvious that in the personal and social problems of today, difficult too in their way, Christians can still hope even as they did. This is a quite different matter from merely dreamily "hoping" that things will change for the better. The Christian's hope is based on the power of God to help him live day by day, confident that God will provide what is needed as his people are faithful to him and do their part.

HYMN In almost every church, there are hymnbooks in the pews. Almost every time Christians gather for worship they participate in the singing of selected hymns. Back of this practice lies a long tradition of the development of the hymnody of the church.

Many of the Old Testament psalms were apparently used in Temple worship or in processions. These continued to be an important part of Christian worship. When the jailer heard Paul and Silas singing in their prison cell at midnight, it would probably have been from The Psalms that they sang. (See Acts 16:25.) At the conclusion of the last supper of Jesus with the apostles, a hymn was sung before they went to the Mount of Olives (Mark 14:26; Matt. 26:30). Perhaps a suggestion as to the worship practice of the early Christian community is contained in Eph. 5:18–19: "Be filled with the Spirit, addressing one another in psalms and hymns and spiritual songs, singing and making melody to the Lord with all your heart" (see also Col. 3:16–17). The earliest use of hymns in the church was accompanied by a mood of joyous thanksgiving.

Soon the Psalter was supplemented with other songs (canticles). Some of these are retained in the New Testament writings, as the Benedictus (Luke 1:68–79), the song of Zechariah at the birth of John the Baptist; the Magnificat (Luke 1:46–55), Mary's song of rejoicing over the coming birth of her child, the Savior; and the Nunc Dimittis (Luke 2:29–32), the song of Simeon, the devout man who took Jesus into his arms at the Temple when Mary and Joseph brought the child for the ceremony of purification. (These titles are the first words of each song in Latin.)

Other hymns soon won their way into general usage in the church. Some have continued to be used throughout the centuries, such as the Te Deum ("We praise thee, O God") and the Benedicite ("O all ye works of the Lord, bless ye the Lord"). For centuries Christians have continued to write poems of prayer and praise. Set to music by talented composers, these constitute the rich heritage of the whole church.

There is a winnowing-out process in the use of hymns. Usually only those survive which express a deep understanding of the Christian faith and have come to be appreciated and used by large numbers of people in the churches.

I

IDOLATRY In many museums are examples of clay or wooden idols such as have been used among various peoples, especially in primitive societies. Sometimes these idols are called "gods." Most historians of religion think that very few people ever actually worshiped the material idol as such, but gave it reverence because for them it was a representation of the deity in which they believed.

Because the Hebrews had faith in one God who was invisible yet all-powerful, it was considered a great sin to try to make any kind of "picture" of God. This was difficult for the people to keep in mind at all times. Written into the Ten Commandments itself was this law: "You shall not make yourself a graven image" (Ex. 20:4). Because many of the other tribes with whom the Hebrews came into contact did have such idols, sometimes they, too, wanted to have them. The prophets constantly had to remind the people that they committed a sin against God whenever they forgot this law. There is a famous story of the way in which Aaron was persuaded by the people to make a golden calf that they might worship. (See Ex., ch. 32.) A typical prophet's reminder is found in Isa. 44:9: "All who make idols are nothing, and the things they delight in do not profit." The writer of Ps. 115 contrasts the one God who is unseen, but who has the power to do as he pleases, with the gods of the heathen: "Their idols are silver and gold, the work of men's hands," etc. (Ps. 115:4–8). Those who worship such idols will be like the gods they worship. Then he calls out: "O Israel, trust in the Lord! He is their help and their shield" (v. 9).

Paul praises the Thessalonians for having turned from idols "to serve a living and true God" (I Thess. 1:9).

But idols are not merely material objects of veneration. Whenever anything else is put in place of God (whether it be an idea, the nation, ambition, or another person or the self), an idol is set up in the heart and mind. Everyone seems to need to have some supreme loyalty in life. As one theologian has put it, "Man has either God or an idol." That to which supreme devotion is given will in the end mold the person like itself. This is why the Christian seeks ever to worship only God as he is known in Jesus Christ. In him alone, true security and meaning for life are to be found.

INCARNATION   "Incarnation" is the term used to refer to God's coming to earth in the person of Jesus. It means literally "becoming flesh" or "taking on the form of a body."

In some types of religion God is thought of as being a great, almighty power that makes and sustains the universe. Because he is so far above men, he can never really be known except as an idea or as an abstract power. He can only be feared and respected.

Christians believe that God is not only the high and holy One who inhabits eternity, but One who took the initiative to come among men in their own flesh and blood so that they might know him and his purposes for them. He did not do this in a general way. He chose to reveal himself in a particular Person who lived in a given time and place, in the historical person, Jesus.

The question arises then, Is Jesus God? The very idea of incarnation implies oneness of God and Jesus. Hence, it would be impossible for the Christian to speak of God at all without speaking of Jesus, and vice versa. But this is not to say that God did not exist before Jesus. The Bible is the record of God's showing himself to many generations of people in the long history of Israel. He was not unknown before Jesus. His mighty works had made him known long before, and the prophets had declared his will for the people. Incarnation means that the God who was active before Jesus now chose to manifest himself in a new and living way to men. The Son was like the Father, but the Father came before the Son. Yet forever after, it was to be only through the Son that men could really know the fullness of the love of God.

"God was in Christ reconciling the world to himself." (II
Cor. 5:19.) That phrase suggests the meaning of incarnation.
"Immanuel" is another word suggesting the same thing: it
means "God is with us." Because God has come into the
world in Jesus, men no longer have to wonder who God is
or merely fear his mighty power. "No one has ever seen God;
the only Son, . . . he has made him known." (John 1:18.)
  See GOD; JESUS CHRIST.

INTERCESSION Intercession means praying for others. It
means to think of other persons in prayer, to remember them
before God and ask his help for them. Sometimes people ask
what good it does to pray for others. Christians believe that
all persons are created by God and thus are precious in his
sight. Since all share in a common humanity, it is not only a
privilege but a duty to pray for others. In intercession one
lays before God the problems, needs, and anything else concerning others with which one would want God to help
them. This does not mean that a person is always able to
understand any fellowman sufficiently to explain to God
what another's needs are; but only, insofar as he is able, to
lay before God the other's concern. The Christian has faith
that God will hear prayer, even though he may not choose
to answer the prayer in the way the petitioner thinks would
be good. One may be wrong in his understanding of what the
other really needs.

  It has been said that intercession is really "courtesy in
prayer." One who prayed only for himself would be selfish
beyond words. All are bound together in mutual concern,
for all are God's children. No one is alone in the common
responsibility to see God's light in the common darkness.
Another way to put it is to say that people should seek to be
like Christ to one another. Each should see the other person
as one for whom Christ lived and died and rose again.

  Even though no one knows how God chooses to help or
guide another for whom he prays, intercession expresses the
trust that God does care for all and that he can do what individuals could never do. Also, in order to pray for another,

one feels goodwill toward him. He is likely to appear more as he does to God himself. That is why Christians are bidden to pray even for their enemies.

Furthermore, Jesus himself gave the example of praying for others. Whether one prays specifically by name for another or not, whenever Christian people say, "Our Father," they are assuming a oneness with all others. It is not *my* Father but *our* one Father who is approached in prayer.

See PRAYER.

ISRAEL   The name Israel refers first of all to Jacob, one of the sons of Isaac, whose life is recounted in the book of Genesis (chs. 25 to 50). There is the familiar story of how he deceives his old father into giving the blessing of the eldest son to him instead of to Esau, to whom it properly belonged. Later, however, Jacob turns into a strong character. In a dream he struggles with the angel of the Lord, saying he will not give up until he receives a blessing from the angel. The Bible says that because of this his name was changed from Jacob ("supplanter," the one who took his brother's rightful place) to Israel ("one who struggles with God"). Jacob's name thus was always to be remembered with the names of Abraham and Isaac as one of the three great patriarchs. Finally, this new name, Israel, was to be used for the whole nation of the Hebrews. They were to be known among the nations as the "Israelites," or "children of Israel," those with whom God entered into a covenant relationship. Today their land is again called Israel, and the inhabitants are referred to as Israeli.

Much later, Christians were to think of themselves as the "New Israel." God, who had entered into covenant with Abraham, Isaac, Jacob, and Moses, was now offering a new covenant with his people, not only with Israel, but with all mankind who would believe. The New Israel was not to be confined to the followers of the old covenant, but was to be made up of all who responded in faith to Jesus Christ, to the end of time.

J

JESUS CHRIST Jesus Christ is the one whom the Christian church calls Lord. God had tried many ways of bringing his people into loving obedience to him, giving them the Law and sending them the prophets. During the time when Augustus Caesar was ruler of the Roman Empire and Herod was king of Judea, God chose to show his nature and purpose to his people in a new way. He took upon himself human form (see INCARNATION) and entered earthly life in the Babe of Bethlehem, Jesus, child of Mary. This does not mean that God's presence and power was limited to this human form; he was still Lord of all his world. But the fullness of God was also seen in Jesus who grew as other children, living in the carpenter's household at Nazareth.

Jesus was about thirty years old when he left Nazareth. He was seen among the crowds following John, a preacher of repentance who was baptizing people as a sign of the forgiveness of their sins. This was in southern Galilee, by the Jordan River. Jesus, too, was baptized, and this seems to have been a sign of a special calling. A Voice said, "Thou art my beloved Son; with thee I am well pleased." (Mark 1:11.) Followers gathered around him as he returned to Galilee. He chose twelve men as special disciples, whom he taught and sent out preaching and healing. His headquarters were in Capernaum, a city near the Sea of Galilee. Wherever he went, crowds gathered. The message he gave them was: "Good news! The rule of God is in your midst." The signs of the Kingdom were the crowds, eager for his words, the healing of the sick, and the casting out of demons (the sign of the conquest of the evil one). Jesus called people to a keeping of the Law, which demanded complete surrender to God. A person could not do this himself: only by the indwelling Spirit of God could such a life be possible.

Jesus' criticism of the leaders among his people, as well

as his own interpretations of the Law, aroused the anger of the leaders. Moreover, they feared that the enthusiastic crowds might bring suspicion from the Roman rulers. Who was this man Jesus? Some said he was a prophet—even the forerunner of the promised Messiah. Others said that he might be the Messiah: one sent of God to free his people from the conquering rule of Rome. When Jesus asked the Twelve who they thought he was, Peter answered, "You are the [Messiah] Christ" (see MESSIAH).

The crowds were turning away, and the rulers were plotting Jesus' downfall. Jesus and his disciples went to Jerusalem for the Passover festival. Surrounded by his followers, he entered the city and taught there each day. At night, alert to the power of his enemies, he stayed with friends in a town several miles away. On Thursday evening of that week, he ate a Passover meal with his disciples. (See LORD'S SUPPER.) That evening he was betrayed by Judas, one of the Twelve, tried before the religious rulers and the Roman governor, and the next day was crucified. But to those who had believed that he was indeed God's Son and the promised One, he appeared, raised from the dead. (See RESURRECTION; EASTER.) Finally, he appeared to a large group of followers, telling them that he was returning to his Father and they would see him no more, but that he would send the Holy Spirit in his place. (See ASCENSION.)

Christians see Jesus' whole life from the perspective of his risen glory. The story of his life is written in four books which are called Gospels, writings setting forth the "good news." Many titles have been given to him. His given name, "Jesus" (in Hebrew, "Joshua"), means "he who saves." The title that his followers use, "Christ" (in Hebrew, "Messiah"), means "one anointed" by God's call. He is known as Son of Man, Son of God, Redeemer, Savior. In his own day he was called "Rabbi," which means "Teacher," and "Master," which means "Lord." But since "Lord" was also the name used to call upon God, the followers of Jesus (after his resurrection) were affirming by the title that there was a special relationship between God and Jesus Christ. Their name for him was "Lord Jesus," and they were willing to live and to die for him because they knew that he had saved them from sin, that he loved them, and that he had given them eternal life.

JUDGMENT On the ceiling of the Sistine Chapel in the Vatican at Rome there is a famous painting by Michelangelo called *The Last Judgment*. In it the Lord is portrayed as sitting on a throne. Before him are throngs of persons awaiting the divine judgment as to how they have used their lives on earth and what shall be their everlasting reward or punishment.

Back of the idea of *The Last Judgment* lies a long history of development. Originally, among earlier peoples, the king was the judge. Since Israel regarded God as superior to all kings, judgment was ascribed to him. His statutes (laws) are contained in the Scriptures and in pronouncements of the rabbis. The prophets insisted on a return to the righteousness demanded by God, and insisted that when Israel disobeyed God, she would be punished. God is the Judge before whom an accounting must be made. Finally, there developed the idea that at some future time there would be a Day of the Lord, when all men, inside as well as outside Israel, would be judged.

Christians inherited the idea of a last judgment. For them Christ (that is, God the Redeemer) became the Judge. It was expected that at the end of time he would come to judge the living and the dead. That expectation was written into the Creeds.

It is not only at the Last Judgment that people will be called on to give an account of their lives. That happens at every stage of life. It is the Christian belief that God knows thoughts and actions, and it is to him that men are responsible at all times. The judgment as to how each has lived his entire life rests with God, but every decision and action helps to shape a total life.

Judgment belongs to God alone. It is not the human privilege to sit in judgment on a fellowman, for no one ever knows the true inner condition of any other human being. It is necessary for governments to establish courts of justice, and individuals must be judged before the law when occasion arises. But in the religious sense no one has any right of judgment over his fellows, although all have the need to help one another grow in righteousness and love.

See RIGHTEOUSNESS.

JUSTIFICATION This important word is sometimes difficult to understand because of the similar English words "just" and "justice." A just person is one who deals rightly and honestly with other persons. Justice is administered by governments; judges are appointed in order to see that fair treatment of all takes place within a society.

The religious word "justification," on the other hand, does not refer to this matter of seeing that justice is carried out. It refers, instead, to the actual relations between persons, the quality of their relationships. Instead of asking, "Am I being justly treated?" the questions are: "Am I in right relationship with the other? Is there anything wrong with the way in which we stand toward each other? Does anything keep us from each other?"

Strictly speaking, justification refers to man's relationship with God. Because of pride, shortcomings, ignorance, and sin, people often separate themselves from God. What can be done to restore a right, loving relationship to him? With other people there are certain things that can be done to restore good relations that have been broken. But toward God there is nothing that one can adequately do to heal the broken relationship.

Some have thought that this could be achieved through works, that is, good deeds of various kinds. Others have said that this can be accomplished by having faith. But human faith is never really great enough to satisfy God's expectations. Even faith could thus be something people themselves produce by trying to have it. No; faith itself is a gift from God. Man can do nothing to be justified before God until he first recognizes that it is God who makes him just. God himself reaches out to forgive and restore. Justification is his gift, always available, but often refused.

This view of justification is given by Paul in his letter to the Romans. At the time of the Protestant Reformation, there came to be a renewed emphasis on justification by faith alone.

Man indeed can do nothing to save himself. He can only be saved by God. Does this mean that there is nothing for man to do at all? At the same time, the saved person is saved for a purpose: that he should be able to live in the world as one who *has* been justified. The book of James in the New Testament suggests that a person of faith will act differently because of what God has done for him. "Faith by itself, if it has no works, is dead." (James 2:17.) In other words, the justified person will himself be just toward others, forgiving, loving, tenderhearted, and merciful.

See JUDGMENT; RIGHTEOUSNESS.

K

KINGDOM OF GOD   Throughout the Gospels, Jesus is shown as having gone about Galilee preaching and teaching the Kingdom of God. In the earliest Gospel, Mark, he announces his work with these words: "The time is fulfilled, and the kingdom of God is at hand; repent, and believe in the gospel" (Mark 1:15).

The phrase "kingdom of God" really means "reign" or "rule" of God. Jesus was not the first to have taught that God must rule in the affairs of men. This conviction was his inheritance from the Jewish religion. The prophets had insisted that God was the righteous One whose will must be obeyed. The whole history of Israel was a turning to and a falling away from the rule of God. Many had resisted having a king over Israel. It was argued that only God could rule Israel. When the monarchy was set up under Saul, it was insisted that the king's power came only because God had anointed him king. The later prophets taught that God's reign would finally come to pass in the whole earth; that sometime a Messiah would appear, sent by God to establish his Kingdom on earth.

By saying "the time is fulfilled," Jesus proclaimed that the reign of God was not something merely to look forward to in the distant future. In that very time, God was breaking through history to establish his Kingdom. Already the Kingdom was appearing. He was calling men to repentance so that they might recognize the rule of God in their personal lives and in society.

Jesus described the nature of the Kingdom in his parables. The Kingdom now at hand would grow slowly, like the seeds put into the ground that finally become the field ripe for harvest. (Mark 4:26–29.) It would be small at first, like the mustard seed, but, like the mustard plant, it would become large when it reached full growth. (Mark 4:30–32.) It is not easy to enter the Kingdom. In order to belong to the Kingdom, a life has to be completely transformed. The Kingdom is already here—we know what God's reign demands—but at the same time it is not completed. Men must continue to pray, "Thy kingdom come," for the completion of the Kingdom is in God's hands and in God's time alone. Yet men are to live now as those who have heard the call of God to enter the Kingdom and to realize in their common life the reign of God. "The kingdom of God is in the midst of you." (Luke 17:21.)

Sometimes one hears people talk about the need for humans to "build the Kingdom of God." That is really not a New Testament way of thinking about the Kingdom. Men do not build the Kingdom. It is declared to them in the Christian gospel. They know what the Kingdom is: the rule of God's love in the hearts and lives of men, the recognition of God's sovereign power over the world and all who are in the world. To build his Kingdom would be an impossible assignment for human beings. But they are to reflect the Kingdom in a way of life, to enter it, to enjoy the eternal life that God's reign offers, and to attract others into the Kingdom by their witness made day by day.

See ETERNAL LIFE; WITNESS.

L

LAITY "Laity" comes from a word meaning "the people." As it is used in the Bible, the Greek word that we translate "laity" or "lay people" means "the people of God." The call of Christians is to be the people of God.

A distinction is usually made in the church between the laity and the ordained ministry. People cease to belong to the laity when they are set apart for special sacramental functions such as the administration of Baptism and the Lord's Supper, and preaching. Lay people also, however, may be set apart for special preaching responsibilities. They are sometimes spoken of as "lay preachers" or "lay readers." In some denominations (e.g., the Baptist, the United Church of Christ, the Methodist) a layman is sometimes authorized to administer the Lord's Supper, usually under such circumstances as when an ordained minister is not available, or if he is being prepared for ordination into the ministry. Baptism may always be administered by a layman in an emergency.

The lay people and clergy together keep the church alive, for the whole church is the worshiping and witnessing community. It is the laity who make up the largest part of the church's membership. It is assumed that at least one other person besides the minister shall be present if the Lord's Supper is to be administered—for minister and congregation together worship God through the sacrament. It is unthinkable that a minister would preach without a congregation. Christian worship is thus a gathering together of the people of God. This is why attendance at worship is not simply a privilege but an obligation for the Christian. The church cannot exist without this gathering. In times of stress and persecution small groups try to gather, even at irregular intervals, in order to know themselves as the people of God. This is a way in which they can strengthen one another in faith. There is no such thing as a solitary Christian. Everyone is a Christian because in some gathering of Christians he or his parents heard the gospel preached, received Baptism, and participated in the Lord's Supper. This is a minimal expression of the faith.

In the twentieth century we think of many functions that lay people perform in the church's life: they teach in church school, belong to church groups, help in money-raising activities, form church committees, sing in choirs, and engage in other important tasks. In some denominations selected lay people are set apart by ordination and/or installation into the lay office of elder or deacon (terms used also in some denominations to indicate orders among clergy—see DEACON; PRESBYTER). By their lives and work they are an example to the church and the world that being a Christian is in itself a calling.

The laity also have an important task in the everyday life of the world. This is where the Christian faith is proclaimed among all men in the lives of those who are called Christian. It is shown in their family life, in their citizenship, and in their attitude toward their work. Where a clergyman sometimes finds it difficult really to know what is going on in the world because people hide their views from him, a lay person knows the extent to which the church is liked or disliked, helpful or harmful, fulfilling its task or ignoring the needs of the culture. Without this insight of the layman, the church could not know how to bring its message to the world.

This is what is meant by Christian witness. Wherever

Christians are at work in all the world, they are demonstrating what Christianity is like, for they are representatives of the church in the world. This is true of a Government worker in India, a businessman in Japan, an assembly-line worker in Detroit, or an office worker in New York. Whether he works in a non-Christian environment or even in a nonreligious environment, the Christian shows forth the kind of people who belong to Christ.

This is why the church cannot exist without the laity, for it is they who bring others into the life of the Christian community. When the church grows in numbers, it is because lay people are accepting their work of telling others by word and deed about the good news of God's love in Christ. If they looked on the church as a kind of private club, it would grow smaller and smaller. They belong to the church only because God has called them to be a part of it.

LAW Law is the rule (remembered orally or written down) by which men are enabled to live at peace with one another in families, communities, and nations. It keeps order even where there is no religious faith. Law comes from the need to regulate relationships among persons and groups of people.

In the Old Testament the Mosaic law is considered to be a gift. Exodus tells how the people of Israel, freed from slavery in Egypt, gathered at Mt. Sinai. There God made a covenant with them, promising to be with them, and gave them the law by which to live in faithfulness to him. (See COVENANT.) The development of the law in Exodus, Leviticus, Numbers, and Deuteronomy covers every area of life, their relationships with other people, the organization of their group, and the ceremonies of their worship. When God chose Israel as his people, he gave them the law both as a pledge of the covenant and as a specific way through which they could express their relationship to him. It set them apart from the people among whom they lived. So the law was precious to

Israel. They celebrated the gift with joy and remembered it with thanksgiving. Many of the psalms refer to the love of God's law. The Feast of Tabernacles (Pentecost) is an annual Jewish celebration in which the people rededicate themselves to the keeping of the law.

There came a time in Israel's history when the law was so overlaid with interpretation that its original intention seemed almost to be forgotten. It became a heavy burden. Jesus objected to this, although saying that he came to fulfill the law (see Matt. 5:17). The law was not meant to make people feel satisfied with themselves. If it was to be truly kept, only God's grace could enable a person to fulfill it.

The apostle Paul found that the harder he tried to keep the law, the less able he was to do so. For him the law was God's way of showing people that they could not live without divine help. It led them to a deeper dependence on God. Then the law, through the guidance of the Holy Spirit, became a guide to obedience. Through the keeping of the law (with God's help) the believer could express his faithfulness and love. The fulfillment of the law would again become a gift and a joy.

LAYING ON OF HANDS   The laying on of hands is an ancient ceremony symbolizing the giving of a blessing, the transfer of a gift, or an appointment to an office. It is used sometimes in the Old Testament, but it has come to us through New Testament usage.

It is written that Jesus laid his hands on the heads of children and blessed them (Mark 10:13–16). He sometimes touched people to heal them.

In The Acts of the Apostles, the laying on of hands often meant the imparting of the gift of the Holy Spirit. This was done by an apostle's laying his hand on the head of a newly baptized person, with the assurance of the gift of the Holy Spirit. (See Acts 2:38.) For some time baptism and the laying on of hands were performed in the same ceremony (combining Baptism and confirmation), as is still the case in the Eastern Orthodox rites. Eventually the laying on of hands was separated from baptism in the Western churches, becoming confirmation at the hands of the bishop only.

This rite was also used by the apostles when seven deacons were chosen to help in the church's work (see Acts 6:6). Since then various office-bearers in the church have been set apart to their functions by the laying on of hands. Whether the offices of elder or deacon be held by laymen or clergymen, those who are elected or appointed to them are set apart in this manner.

In churches of the Catholic tradition the laying on of hands is an important symbol in the consecration of bishops. For them this signifies the transfer of the authority from the original apostles to those in each generation who have been called to the office of bishop. It symbolizes the continuity of the history, tradition, and activity of the church through these men who are elected to preserve and to carry forward the work of proclaiming the gospel. (See BISHOP.)

See CONFIRMATION; ORDINATION.

LENT Lent is a period set apart as a preparation for Easter. The word comes from the "lengthening" of the days as spring approaches. The number of days in this preparatory period varied during the first few centuries of the church, but finally became established as forty days, symbolizing the period during which Jesus was tempted in the wilderness just before beginning his public ministry. Since Sundays were always feast days of the resurrection, they were not included in the forty days of penitence. Thus the actual time of Lent is forty-six days.

In early centuries it was a time of preparation for baptism. Those who desired to become Christians were involved in an educational preparation in the meaning of the Christian faith. Baptism itself took place on Easter Eve. Those already Christians shared in this preparation by deepening their awareness of the meaning of faith and by actions that would make them more ready to take part in the events of Holy Week and Easter.

Lent became a time for thinking of their sinfulness, of

seeking a deeper level of repentance, of trying with God's help to reach a new intensity of Christian living. They came to Holy Week with an awareness of the necessity for God's action in order that man could be redeemed. Aware of sin, they were also able to rejoice deeply in the deliverance from sin made sure in the resurrection of Jesus Christ the Lord.

Sometimes the deeper meaning of Lent has become lost today in petty things such as the "giving up" of habits that some people fully intend to resume after Easter. Such attempts to prove that one can go without certain things can be both temporary and negative. Lent is meant to be a reorientation of life around one's baptismal vows, so that the Christian may more truly and sincerely participate in both the death and resurrection of Christ, signified for him once in his Baptism, and continually as he takes part in the Lord's Supper.

LITURGY The word "liturgy" brings up a picture of a ceremony. Actually the word comes from the Greek, meaning "common work." Perhaps the nearest word to it in English is "service." We speak of the "church service," or the "service of worship." This is what liturgy means. For worship is work and service. It is a giving of ourselves to God.

When the service of worship is looked at in this way, one can see that it is not a sort of performance in which a clergyman does certain things and says certain words while the people sit back and listen. It is a work for God in which minister and lay people all have their parts. Some of it is done responsively: versicles and psalms, for instance. Some is done in unison: hymns and some prayers. In the reading of the Scriptures and in preaching, the minister speaks; the people respond by listening to the preacher's words as he seeks to interpret God's Word to man. In the offering, the congregation give to God a part of that which he has enabled them to earn during the week. This is their thanksgiving to him and their acknowledgment that all things come from him. The clergyman receives and dedicates this offering.

When the minister speaks the prayers, it is in order that all may follow together the words and all pray together in attitudes of praise, thanksgiving, intercession, and petition.

Liturgy as common work can be clearly seen in the celebration of the Lord's Supper. It was an old custom for the people to bring the bread as their offering. The clergyman received it, blessed it, and used it in the service. Now the people sing ancient hymns together, such as the Sanctus and the Gloria in Excelsis Deo. They rise to confess their mutual faith in the words of one of the Creeds. Lay people and clergy both receive the bread and the cup. They pray together in the words of the Lord's Prayer. The Eastern Orthodox Churches actually call the Lord's Supper by the name "The Liturgy." In their celebrations the ceremony is most elaborate, sometimes taking several hours, during which the people stand. There are music, incense, ornate vestments—sound, movement, fragrance, and color. In some Protestant denominations the Lord's Supper can be seen in its simplest form. It may consist merely of the reading of the words of institution at the Last Supper from First Corinthians, a prayer by a deacon, and the distribution of the bread and the cup among the people.

All churches have been concerned about the degree of participation by the people in the liturgy. The fact that a liturgy is simple does not necessarily mean that the people take much part; often they are only listeners, the minister doing most of the speaking. An elaborate liturgy may become, to outward view, a spectacle. But for a liturgy to be a truly Christian work in worship, the people must not only see and hear, but respond, in words and action. When they leave their work of worship in the church building, they are ready to begin the expression of their worship in the daily work they do in the world.

See CEREMONY; RITUAL.

LORD   "Lord" is the word that the Old Testament frequently uses to refer to God. The name of God was thought to be sacred; hence his people addressed him as Lord. This term is a reminder that man may not be "familiar" with God, even though he is loved by God and can return that love. The word "dominion" comes from a Latin word that means "lordship." The lord is the one who holds power (dominion) over other beings.

The word has been used also to indicate the ruler and the ruled. It establishes the relationship between king and people, master and slave. Whatever lordship man may have over other men is both paralleled by the Lordship of God and derived from his dominion. Because God is the Lord, he can grant to men certain powers over other men. Whenever used without reference to the Lordship of God, such power is evil.

The New Testament takes the word "Lord" as used for God and applies it to Jesus. In the Gospels he is simply Lord in the sense of a master who has chosen disciples to be with him. But those who knew him in the power of his resurrection began to realize that they had met God in him. In one of the letters (Rom. 10:13) Paul takes an Old Testament reference to God as Lord and applies it to Jesus. Christians believed that in Jesus Christ they saw God acting in a special way; thus the word they had always applied to God, they now applied to Jesus. He was also lord of the church, his special people; he was their Head. He was Lord to each individual Christian who had promised in Baptism to be faithful and obedient. Paul does not hesitate to call himself the slave of Christ. This is what it meant to call Jesus "Lord": that one would both live and die for him as a witness that God was in him.

LORD'S DAY   The Lord's Day is Sunday. Christians have always gathered on the first day of the week as a reminder of the Resurrection Day. Thus each Sunday is a little Easter: a festival day and a day of rejoicing.

This makes it somewhat different in emphasis from Saturday, the Jewish Sabbath. The keeping of the Sabbath derives from the Eighth Commandment (see Ex., ch. 20; Deut., ch. 5) and from the first chapter of Genesis; the Sabbath is the last day of the week, signifying that God rested after his work of creation. It is a day in remembrance of creation (and later of deliverance from Egypt; see Deut. 5:15). In accordance with ancient custom the day lasts from sundown (Friday) to sundown (Saturday).

Sunday, however, following later calendar custom, extends from midnight to midnight. In remembrance of the dawn discovery of the resurrection, Christians in the first century worshiped at an early hour. Since many of them were slaves, this was the only time at which they could slip away to join fellow Christians at worship. The custom of early worship has been continued in many Christian groups, and Sunday morning is the usual time for the service.

Although the Old Testament has careful laws concerning the keeping of the Sabbath, the New Testament makes no prescriptions as to how the Lord's Day is to be observed. Several Gospel narratives suggest that although Jesus faithfully attended the synagogue on the Sabbath, he overstepped some of the interpretations of the law regarding how one "worked" on that day. The idea that "the Sabbath was made for man, not man for the sabbath" (Mark 2:27) has generally carried over into the Christian observance of the Lord's Day. However, some Christian groups have added the Old Testament idea of the Sabbath to the observance of the Lord's Day, making it a day of rest, and sometimes severely restricting the activity of the day.

The Lord's Day is not understood in its intent, however, if it is not a weekly remembrance with joy of Christ's resurrection.

LORD'S PRAYER "The Lord's Prayer" is the name given to the prayer that Jesus gave to his disciples (see Matt. 6:9–13; Luke 11:2–4). The prayer opens with praise to God and a petition for the coming of his rule; it continues with personal petitions for food and deliverance from evil. In Matthew's Gospel it ends with a doxology, "For thine is the kingdom," but this is omitted in Luke, which is generally considered to be the older form.

The words of this prayer as they have come to us in the Gospels are a remembrance of the oral tradition handed down from the first generation of the church. Since this prayer was given to the disciples, it belongs to the gathering of the people of God in the church. It was never meant to belong to society in general, but to be a part of Christian worship and devotion.

The prayer lifts up the petitions of greatest concern to Christian people: that God's Kingdom may come and his will be done; that his people may be cared for and protected. It raises their praise of God, the Holy One.

Individual Christians have used it as part of their personal devotion, meditating on its meanings and finding in it a pattern for prayer. Whether used privately or corporately, it is a reminder that all Christians are bound together in Christ, their Lord, who gave them these words for worship.

The outline is brief, yet many books have been written on the meaning of each petition. "Our Father" suggests a Christian understanding of God (Father) and implies a group at worship (our). "Who art in heaven" indicates that God, who may be addressed by an earthly name, is above the earth he has created. "Hallowed be thy name" refers to the holiness of God, whose name may not be spoken lightly because of who he is. "Thy kingdom come" is the petition borne out by the words and work of Jesus, in whose person the rule of God was breaking into human existence. The petition for bread suggests that all man's needs may be placed before God, who provides for his creatures. The prayer for deliverance from evil (or the evil one) is the Christian's hope that in all times of testing he may be faithful to his Lord.

Although the prayer is taught to little children, people spend lifetimes meditating on its range and depth of meaning.

See PRAYER.

LORD'S SUPPER The Lord's Supper is the church's commemoration of the meal that Jesus and the Twelve shared on the night before his crucifixion. That Last Supper took place during the Passover season. Jesus seems to have made a connection between God's deliverance of his people from Egypt, which that festival celebrates, and God's new salvation, about to take place in his own death and resurrection. The Last Supper is described in Matt. 26:17–35; Mark 14:12–31; and Luke 22:7–38. In I Cor. 11:23–26 Paul describes the tradition that had been given to him. Paul's account is the earliest written one. Like the other three accounts, it had been received by him as part of the oral tradition, and doubtless had been told in the churches for many years before being recorded.

There are several emphases in the Lord's Supper. It is a memorial. Jesus said, "Do this in remembrance of me." He was going to his death, but he commanded his disciples that when they gathered together they were to break the bread and drink from the cup, remembering him. Moreover, it is a witness to him. It was a proclamation of his death. "For as often as you eat this bread and drink the cup, you proclaim the Lord's death until he comes." (I Cor. 11:26.) It also points to his return to his people. In the words of the Gospel, "I shall not drink again of the fruit of the vine until that day when I drink it new in the kingdom of God." (Mark 14:25.)

The Lord's Supper is also a reminder of Christ's sacrificial death. "This is my body." The new covenant is the redemption from sin through Christ, and the eternal life that he gives. But because he rose from the dead, and has commanded his disciples to continue the Supper, it is also the sign of his continuing presence. "For where two or three are gathered in my name, there am I in the midst of them." (Matt. 18:20.) This is indicated in several of the resurrection narratives: the disciples from Emmaus recognized him in the breaking of bread (Luke 24:13–32); he appeared to the disciples by the shore of the Sea of Tiberias (John 21:1–14), and in the upper room at Jerusalem (Luke 24:36–43). Thus the sharing of the bread and wine in the Lord's Supper was always a distinctive sign of the disciples' meeting in the presence of their Lord.

The Lord's Supper has always had a strong note of rejoicing and thanksgiving. It is a reminder, not only of Jesus' death, which brought freedom from the bondage of sin, but of his resurrection, which makes him the Lord of life. As the liturgies developed, the note of thanksgiving was always important.

The celebration of the Lord's Supper has continued to be a major part of the church's worship since the first years of the church's life. In some parts of Christendom the sacrament of the Lord's Supper is observed daily; in other parts, as seldom as four times a year. The sacrament has been called by various names: the Holy Communion (suggesting his presence), the Eucharist (thanksgiving), the Holy Mysteries (his spiritual presence). (See SACRAMENT.) The various names suggest and emphasize one of the many notes always present in the event. The forms of the rite have varied greatly in different parts of the church around the world, but they are always a continuing link with the historic presence of Jesus among his disciples, his living presence with the church today, and his promise that he will be with his people until the end of the world.

LOVE   The Bible uses the word "love" primarily to refer to the love of God. Throughout the Old Testament there is the assertion that God chose Israel to be his people, showing his love to them through his continual guidance. This is a personal love, given to Israel, not because it was deserved or earned, but simply because the nature of God is love and he wished to have a people to love.

While Israel could claim God's love because he had made a covenant with them, nevertheless the continuation of the relationship always involved righteousness. God's love is not sentimental; it is holy. (See HOLINESS.) The sin of his people constantly separated them from God, and he alone could forgive and restore them. They frequently worshiped other gods; they oppressed their own people; they forgot the covenant. But God recalled them to himself; he could bring them to repentance.

Although the Old Testament thinks of Israel collectively, as a people, it is also aware that God's love is made known to individuals as members of this people. The individual's love for God is a response to the realization that God loves him. It is expected that he can show his love for God in the way he treats other people, acting in justice and mercy. This love is shown first to those of his own people, but the Old Testament also commands people to show love to the stranger living among them, and sometimes to the enemy.

In the writings of the New Testament the love of God is known in Jesus Christ. His love is made known in the very act of sending the divine Son into the world. It is made evident in the actions of Jesus: sharing the life of men, showing love and mercy, feeding, healing, and assuring them of God's love. It is shown in his dying and in his rising. The purpose of God in the crucifixion and resurrection of Jesus was to reconcile men to himself so that they could respond to his love. Jesus was the embodiment (incarnation) of the love of God. When he left the disciples, the gift of the Holy Spirit (at Pentecost) was the continuation of the love of God in the life of the people of the new covenant, the church. God's love is holy, and it makes holy those who receive it into their lives. It can be rejected, but it is always freely offered. In the New Testament, as in the Old Testament, the nature of God is portrayed throughout as love.

Human love is the response to this unfailing love of God. It is an overflowing of the divine love in human relationships. First it is the human response to God's love: "We love, because he first loved us" (I John 4:19). Then it is a response to other human beings because of the assurance of the love of God: "Beloved, if God so loved us, we also ought to love one another" (I John 4:11). In the work of the disciples throughout the Roman world, this basic outreach of love as indicated in the epistles was proclaimed and shown to all men.

The Bible is clear that it is useless for men to talk about the love of God if they are not showing it in human relationships. Evil in the world will always threaten that love—the crucifixion is an example of this—but God's love is greater than human evil. The final triumph of the love of God will be known only in his own time. Sin brings judgment—both in the present moment and in the hour of ultimate judgment—and this judgment is placed within the holy love of God. All human love is derived from his love and can exist because of it.

M

MAN   Man has been examined from many points of view. The scientist can measure him physically, intellectually, psychologically, and within his environment. The philosopher asks questions about man's life in an effort to understand man's being and existence.

If you were to ask someone, "Who are you?" the answer would not come in terms of weight or psychological type, but by the giving of your own name and address. Man is known in terms of his relationships: family, friends, working place, and nation.

Man is created by God. Everything to be said about man stems from this fact. The subject of the Bible is God's dealings with man in the light of this special relationship between them. Because God created man, man is totally dependent upon God. The nature of this relationship, however, derives from the reason for God's creating man, namely, to have living creatures to respond to his love. "So God created man in his own image." (Gen. 1:27.) This "image" is the ability to know love, goodness, and righteousness.

The word "Adam" comes from the Hebrew meaning "man." The story of Adam and Eve is the story of mankind, rather than that of a particular man and woman. Man was created righteous by God. He was created to receive and respond to the love of God. He was made "little less than God" (Ps. 8:5), and was granted rule over the rest of God's creation.

But man was also created with the freedom to make choices. His desire to rule himself led to the disobedience that changed his life. (See FALL.) Thus man became a sinner: one who could receive and respond to the love of God, but also one who could turn away from that love to do evil and to feel hatred.

Because man is human and not divine, his life is limited and he dies. This marks the boundaries of his striving and achievement, of the good that he can do and the evil. He is not God to rule the earth eternally.

Man is the prodigal son who has left the Father's house with his inheritance. Yet however selfishly man uses his will, he is never far from his Father's house. He can return, and the Father will receive the repentant son.

The New Testament sees Christ as the New Adam, the one who lived in perfect obedience and surrender to God. Through him mankind has been offered the gift of eternal life, which is the attribute of God himself.

Man is the one through whom God makes his work known in the world in a particular way. The natural world reveals the creative work of God in many ways. Man, able to reflect the love of God, can show something of the nature of God by the way in which he exercises his rule over God's earth. He is responsible to God for the way in which he uses the earth (land, air, and sea) and for the way in which he acts toward all living creatures of earth. Through their actions men reflect the image of God in their lives. This image, when distorted by selfish desire, acts in sinful ways that harm God's creation. But indwelt by the Holy Spirit, man can become a part of God's redemptive work, fulfilling the purpose of God for his world.

See CREATION; REDEMPTION.

MARRIAGE   The Biblical view of marriage has been summed up in the words of Genesis, "Male and female he created them" (Gen. 1:27), with the addition made by Jesus, "The two shall become one" (Mark 10:8). Marriage holds out the possibility that a man and woman shall have a complete existence through life together.

The Old Testament assumed a marriage pattern in which a man has more than one wife: polygyny. This was done to assure the continuity of the family, for children and grandchildren were then considered to be a man's one hope of remembrance. Abraham took Hagar as his wife in addition to Sarah, because Sarah had no children. Plural marriage enlarged the tribal group, and so increased its possibilities for survival.

This pattern continued until the time of the exile (fourth century B.C.), but in the New Testament another pattern is given: that a man have one wife. The husband is the head of the wife, but there is to be a relationship of mutual giving, best symbolized by the relationship between Christ and his church (see Eph. 5:21–33). Divorce is not permitted (it was in the Old Testament). If a Christian married to a pagan was divorced, the Christian was to remain unmarried. The church reacted strongly against the casual attitude toward marriage to be seen in the cities of the Roman world. They recalled that the Old Testament prophet Hosea had likened the relationship of God to his people Israel in terms of a loving husband forgiving an unfaithful wife. Even when Israel was faithless to God, he remained with her, loving and strengthening her, and desiring to restore the relationship between them.

Christian marriage is founded on Christian love. The love that Christians know from God is a saving love. Where this exists, there is no question of resolving a marriage. Without it, a marriage is not Christian anyway. The New Testament point of view has been normative in the church. Christian marriage has been a form of Christian witness in the world, particularly in non-Christian countries.

MARTYR The word "martyr" comes from a Greek word meaning "witness." There have been martyrs for many causes. In present usage a martyr is a person whose witness leads to his death. The days in the Christian calendar that commemorate those who witnessed unto death have red as their liturgical color, thus marking the heroic men and women of Christian history.

The Christian martyr is one who dares to confess his faith in Christ, even when this would lead to danger. Each Christian at his Baptism or confirmation promises to accept Christ as his Lord and to confess him before men. The Christian life is not difficult within the Christian community. However, life can be difficult indeed for the person who tries to live differently from those around him and who is ridiculed and resented. Trying to explain his faith and at the same time being ridiculed is difficult too. There come times of crisis when the Christian church seems so dangerous to an existing order that the government tries to suppress it. This is accomplished by ordering Christians to renounce their faith and by imprisoning, torturing, and/or killing those who persist in their confession of Christ. That is the most difficult action that can be asked of a person. Many, of course, have failed, and have been forgiven their failure. Others have accepted death. During the first three centuries of the church, every persecution was followed by increased numbers of persons desiring to be baptized. The final widespread persecution, which lasted intermittently for fifty years all over the empire, ended with a proclamation of tolerance. Eventually, Christianity became the accepted religion of the Roman Empire.

Martyrdom has never ceased to be a possibility within the life of the Christian church. The present century has seen martyrdom in Russia during attempts to make the country atheistic; in Nazi Germany in an attempt to force the church to form itself as the government wished; and in African countries, in their struggles for independence, when "Christian" is sometimes identified with "Western." Among the

Jews, there have been more people who died because of their faith in this century than in all previous centuries put together.

See WITNESS.

MARY   The Bible has few references to Mary, the mother of Jesus. On one occasion, when he was addressing a crowd, word was brought to him that his mother and brothers wanted to speak to him. But he replied, looking at his hearers, that those who heard and did the will of God were his mother and brothers. (See Mark 3:31–35.) Another time, the skeptical people at Nazareth, after hearing him teach in the synagogue, said: "Is not this the carpenter's son? Is not his mother called Mary? And are not his brothers James and Joseph and Simon and Judas? And are not all his sisters with us?" (Matt. 13:55–56).

The Gospel According to John tells how Jesus and his disciples attended a wedding feast at Cana. His mother asked him to change water into wine so that the host would not be embarrassed by an insufficient supply. (John 2:3–5.)

Mary, the mother, stood at the foot of the cross when all but one of the disciples had left him. In the tradition of the Fourth Gospel, Jesus commends her to the care of the apostle John, who stood beside her in those terrible hours (John 19:26–27). She is also mentioned among those who, after the ascension of Jesus, met together for prayer in an upper room at Jerusalem, awaiting the coming of the Holy Spirit (Acts 1:14).

The theological discussion about the mother of Jesus arises from the stories of his birth, found in Matthew and Luke. Here it is said that before her marriage to Joseph, an angel appeared to tell her that she had been chosen by God to be the mother of Jesus, who would save his people from their sins. Her reply of perfect and simple obedience to the purpose of God has elevated her as the symbol of faithfulness. Unmindful of what people would say, she accepted this work of the Holy Spirit. She was married to Joseph, went with him to his ancestral town of Bethlehem to fulfill the requirement of the Roman government for an enrollment of all the people, and there her son was born.

The story of the virgin birth does not prove that Jesus was the divine Son of God so much as it simply reflects the fact. Because his followers had seen the saving power of God in the crucified and risen Jesus, they preserved this story of a wonderful birth. For the true wonder lies in the fact that God would come to live among men in human form at all. How he came could never quite match that mystery. So the Virgin Mary, mother of Jesus, God made man, is honored in the church. Eve, the mother of mankind, disobeyed God, and brought sin into the world. Mary, the second Eve, gave God perfect obedience, and in fulfilling her work, made possible the fulfillment of God's redeeming purpose for the world.

MEDIATOR Although the word "mediator" appears only a few times in the New Testament, the idea of the mediator is a part of Biblical thought. The covenant of the Old Testament assumes a mediator. Abraham and, later, Moses, are persons who mediate the covenant between God and Israel. This form of mediation comes down from God to man, as a way by which a relationship may be established between them. Later in the Biblical history, there develops a mediation through the priests and the sacrifices of Tabernacle and Temple—a way of mediation through which man reaches up toward God, reestablishing the relationship already made by God in the covenant. These two movements are both found in the Prophets. The word of the prophet, "Thus saith the Lord," was a word from above; the intercession of the prophet was a word from man to God.

The church, reflecting on the life and work of Jesus Christ, found him to be *the* Mediator. He gave his life that man might reach toward God. At the same time, God was acting in him, reaching toward man and seeking a new relationship with his children.

A mediator is one who stands in the middle to bring two

people or two groups together. So Christ the Mediator stands midway between God and man. The letter to the Hebrews takes this as its theme. He was sent by God to reveal God's purpose, to deliver men from sin, and to bring them the gift of eternal life. Yet he is not only the representative of God. He is also the representative of man. Through his earthly life and the giving up of himself to death he is able to be the sacrifice. So God, in both his divine and his human aspects, acts to save his people from sin and death and to bring them eternal life. This is the nature of the new covenant. Jesus Christ, God and man, is its perfect Mediator.

MERCY The word "mercy" means "loving-kindness" and is used, mostly in the Old Testament, for God's kindness and favor toward his people. It occurs more often in The Psalms than anywhere else in the Bible. It is seldom used in the New Testament.

The word "mercy" does not refer to the forgiveness of sins, and it can be understood quite apart from this need. Mercy is simply the kindness of God, the expression of his love. It does not depend on anything man does. It is an expression of the nature of God. It is God's pity toward man's misery and helplessness. Although there are occasional references to mercy in connection with atonement and forgiveness, this is not the primary use of the word in the Bible.

Today the word is used also to refer to attitudes of human beings. Such a use takes a word that was originally connected with the divine nature alone and puts it to human use. Since mercy is an expression of God, the mercy shown to others by a human being would be an expression of the Spirit of God in his life. It still carries the same meaning when used this way: showing kindness or favor, without regard to the merit of those to whom it is shown.

MESSIAH "Messiah" comes from a Greek word meaning "the anointed one." It is used more often in the Old Testament than in the New Testament. In the former it has a definite meaning: the anointed one is the person who has been set apart for the service of God, either as priest or king. As such he had been called by God.

Centuries later, after Israel had returned from the exile and was being oppressed by the Greek Empire, writers began to think of the Messiah as one whom God would call to restore the Kingdom of Israel. The people in Jesus' day knew of this hope, and the disciples wondered if he were the one so chosen. It is generally thought that he never told them in what way he thought of himself as Messiah, if at all.

The prophet known as the Second Isaiah, writing in the period of the exile, had drawn the picture of a Suffering Servant of God who would restore Israel. This was quite different from the popular picture of the Messiah as a conquering king.

Although there is little mention of the Messiah in the New Testament, the idea has persisted within the church that Jesus was, in some way, the one chosen by God to save his people. To the Christian he appears as one who has saved them from sin and restored them to eternal life. Thus "Messiah" is one of the names (or titles) given to Jesus.

The Greek word for Messiah is *Christos,* which we translate "Christ." Sometimes it is used before the given name (Christ Jesus), sometimes after it (Jesus Christ), each usage meaning the same thing. The origin of these different ways of referring to him is vague. Another Greek word, *chrēstos,* pronounced almost the same way as *Christos,* means "kind." Possibly non-Christian, referring to Jesus, it meant to say "kind Jesus." On the other hand, the term "Messiah" would have had meaning for Jewish Christians. Soon the term "Christ" became scarcely more than a part of his name, though it has continued to point out to Christians the lofty calling of the one who was anointed by God for his work of salvation of mankind.

MINISTRY The word "ministry" means a "service"; a minister is one who serves. The church's use of the word comes from an incident in the Gospels (see Mark 10:35–45). Jesus, teaching the disciples, says that he who is greatest among them will be one that serves, even as the "Son of man also came not to be served but to serve, and to give his life as a ransom for many" (Mark 10:45).

All Christians are part of a common ministry to one another and to the world. They serve one another in mutual helpfulness and strengthening. They serve the world by witnessing in words and life to the good news. Some Christian groups highlight this fact by insisting that every member is a minister, and that no one is ordained in a special way to a particular form of ministry.

However, from the earliest days of the church, as one learns from The Acts of the Apostles and the letters, there were specific offices in the church. Some offices were held by those with special gifts—for teaching, healing, preaching. Others were held because persons were chosen and set apart for the tasks involved. The laying on of hands was the special way by which authority for a specific task was granted to a person. (See LAYING ON OF HANDS.) The New Testament mentions the apostles, chosen by Christ (Paul considers himself also to have been so chosen), deacons (first chosen by the apostles at Jerusalem), presbyters, or elders, and bishops, or overseers. It was not until the second century that these various offices came to have a definite and uniform order. (See APOSTLE; BISHOP; DEACON; PRESBYTER.)

The Old Testament tells about the ministry of the priests who perform the sacrifices in the Temple. The priests belonged to the tribe of Levi. The prophets felt themselves to be individually called by God to proclaim his word. When the synagogue arose during the exile as a place of worship and study, its functions were all performed by laymen. Any man might be called upon to read and explain the Scriptures (as Jesus was in his time, and Paul in various synagogues he visited). The ruler of the synagogue, who took charge of its affairs, was also a layman. When the Temple was restored at Jerusalem, the priesthood of the tribe of Levi also was restored. The scribes were laymen who interpreted the law; the rabbis were teachers.

The apostles seem to have had a special place in the life of the church. As they established congregations in many places throughout the Roman Empire, elders were left in charge of each congregation. The administration of the Lord's Supper introduced a new note in worship, which (in Jewish congregations) had consisted of Scripture, interpretation, and prayers. The thanksgiving and blessing, which corresponded to Jesus' own action at the Last Supper, were given by the person especially chosen to preside.

Particular functions in the church during the apostolic period were carried on by persons who were deemed to possess clear gifts of the Holy Spirit. These persons were chosen and set apart, often by the apostles, for certain offices. Thus the needs were met as they arose: for the conduct of worship, teaching, and the care of the poor. Except in the case of the apostles themselves, who may have given most or all of their time to this work, this was a ministry of men who carried on their daily work in the world. Only the apostles were cared for at the expense of the whole church (and Paul says that he supported himself at his trade of tentmaking). The full-time ministry arose when the churches grew large enough to need it—first bishops (or overseers), who had charge of the congregations in an area (see BISHOP), then teachers, and eventually pastors of individual churches.

The New Testament is always clear on this point: any ministry was a gift of the Holy Spirit, and the person who exercised it had been chosen by God to do so.

MIRACLE　The Bible uses three different words for "miracle." A miracle can be a mighty work (power), a wonder, or a sign. Usually a miracle is regarded as a manifestation of the mighty power of God. It demonstrates that God is Lord of the natural world that he has made and ruler over the history of the events of mankind.

The basic miracle of the Old Testament is the deliverance of the people of Israel from Egypt, and specifically the crossing of the Red Sea. The question here should not concern how wide the sea was or how deep or how fiercely the winds were blowing at the time. To the Hebrew people, this was a historical event that so impressed itself upon them that it was remembered and retold in every household, and was the basis for one of their most sacred holy days. Passover signifies not only the passing over of the angel of death (whereas the Egyptians were not spared), but also the safe passage over the Red Sea. (See PASSOVER.) The significance of the event, however it came about physically, was that God controlled historical events. By his mighty power God could free his people and send them toward the land that he had promised them. This ability thus to fulfill his promise and to reaffirm his covenant with them was an indication that God was the Lord.

The basic New Testament miracle is the resurrection of Christ. If the church had not been sure of that event, there would have been no need to remember other actions of Jesus. The resurrection was an action of God by which he showed his power over sin and death. This is the sense in which it is a mighty work. Again, it determined the course of historical, human events.

The healings of Jesus were signs that the presence (and power) of God was working among men in the person of Jesus. These healings took place only in response to faith. Note that the healed persons were not indicating specifically the faith that Jesus would heal, but more basically a faith that because he was God's chosen one, he *could* heal. The faith was in Jesus himself. The healing was a response to this faith in Jesus. What Jesus expected to happen when people saw such a mighty work was not that they would say, "How wonderful this man is!" but, rather, that they would say, "God is among us!" They would then repent of their sins and turn to serve God. This is indicated in passages where he rebukes them because signs of the mighty power of God were supposed to lead to a sense of sin and to repentance, but the people merely looked and said, "Who is this?" So the miracles were never meant to "prove" anything about the person of Christ. They were meant to convert. This was the purpose of remembering and retelling the stories and finally of writing them down in the New Testament Gospels.

The so-called "nature" miracles were a recognition by the disciples that the power of God was being shown in their midst, for in The Psalms they read that God commanded the sea, and it obeyed. The feeding of the multitude showed how God provided for his people. (It has also been suggested that in the feeding of the multitude there is an action with which the disciples were familiar on many occasions: that he took bread and blessed it, and gave it to them.)

The mighty works of Jesus were understood only by those whose eyes were open to believe and whose ears were open to hear. Sometimes, in the Gospel stories, an incident where Jesus heals blindness is followed by one in which he points out the spiritual blindness of the disciples to whom he speaks or one where he heals deafness and asks, "Have you not ears to hear?" Spiritual blindness and deafness were more difficult to cure than physical handicap, and the cure was as much a miracle.

So the questions regarding the mighty works of God in the Bible are not historical—Did it happen? or What exactly did happen? The Gospel records are as accurate as any writings of their time. They are not interested in the same kind of reporting that concerns the twentieth century. The question regarding the miracles is: What is the meaning of this event? The meaning is that God is showing his power through Jesus Christ in order that men, hearing and seeing, may repent, turn from their own ways, and serve him. As such they are signs and witness.

MISSION   Mission indicates the task of the Christian church. The word means "sent out." The mission of the church has its beginning in the command of the risen Lord to his disciples, "Go therefore and make disciples of all nations" (Matt. 28:19). The Christian church is sent out into the whole world. This means that the work of the church is not confined within the four walls of a building. The mission of the church is in the world. The church gathers to worship God, their Redeemer and Lord, and goes out to do the work that he commands. This is the work of demonstrating the good news that God has shown his love to his children by sending Jesus into the world. It is the promise of the forgiveness of sins and the gift of eternal life.

This mission begins outside the doors of the church in the neighborhood in which the church lives. It spreads from there into the surrounding city or country. It extends into all the land and then across national borders and beyond the oceans into all the world.

Sometimes the good news is told in words. Sometimes it is put in pictures to be seen or books to be read. Sometimes it is shown in the lives that Christians live toward their neighbors. People who see and hear them can get a clearer idea of what they mean by "good news."

Many Christians today travel into all parts of the world, either on business or for pleasure. They are always on the mission of the church, although sometimes they forget this. They are showing the meaning of Christ in the way they act toward people whom they may meet anywhere. On the other hand, many Christians never leave their own town, city, or country. They too take part in the mission of the church. They do so by the money that they give to support the worldwide mission of the church, and by the interest they show in fellow Christians who are actively engaged as their representatives in doing this work. They do so by their participation in the life of their own country, which stands, in the eyes of the world, as a Christian country. Even their voting suggests how the gospel is shown around the world.

The mission of the church is carried out through the seriousness with which members try to meet the problems within their own country, whether it be the needs of families, concern for racial equality, or voting for honorable candidates in elections. All responsible people engage in these activities, but when the Christian does so, he tells the world that the church is concerned because it is the church of God. The purpose of this type of witness is in order that people who are indifferent to or even opposed to Christianity may at least believe that Christians do not live only for one another but for all. In doing this, they are showing themselves to be like their Lord, whose concern was to bring all men into the Kingdom of his Father.

The mission of the church is to the world's need. Sometimes it consists in showing the world that it has needs, making it discontented with things as they are. Only thus can the need for God be known and the Spirit of God enter into the area of need.

Each Christian is a missionary. It is his task to carry on the mission of the church in his personal life and as a member of the church.

See APOSTLE; WITNESS.

MYSTERY   A mystery is something hidden. In common usage, a mystery is something unclear that eventually will be solved. We say, "That is a mystery," meaning that we do not know why it happened or what was involved in its occurrence. Mystery, here, is ignorance. Careful seeking will bring the answers.

The Old Testament never used the word "mystery," but it is found in the New Testament. Here the mystery is the unknown because it is hidden. It is a secret, and God has not revealed (that is, uncovered) the meaning. (See REVELATION.) The Gospels speak of the Kingdom of God as a mystery. Man knows not when or how it comes, but in God's time the Kingdom appears in his midst. The divine purpose —God's plan of salvation—has been hidden, but now in Christ it is made known.

The apostle Paul uses the word in another way: to describe that which is so wonderful as to overwhelm his understanding. The entrance of the Gentiles into God's plan, which originally included only the chosen people, is that kind of mystery to Paul.

The response to the divine mystery is not intensive probing by the human understanding. Rather, it is awe and wonder, patient waiting, until God makes known his purpose to men. Those who believe have their eyes opened and they can see. The hidden is made clear, and they are enabled to respond to the gospel.

N

NAME   An individual's name belongs to him in a most personal way. He has a family name, common to a group of people, but his Christian, or given, name specifies him as one particular person.

In the Bible, God has a name, "Yahweh." Since God is holy, his name also is sacred, and is not often used. The earliest narratives use the name, but later ones do not. The completed manuscripts as we have them most often use the name "Lord" or "Lord God." Since Yahweh has now been interpreted as God, that word, with the capital *G*, has become, in our language, a proper (or personal) name.

Each individual has a surname. No one stands alone, but is part of a family; thus the family name is used with the given, or individual, name. In the Old Testament we read of Isaac, son of Abraham; or Solomon, son of David. This custom of naming sons after their fathers survives in modern surnames such as Johnson (John's son).

In addition to the family name, there is the personal name by which a man is called and which marks him as an individual. Within the Christian community it is the name given at Baptism (whether infant or adult) whereby one is named in the presence of God as belonging to God in a special way through Jesus Christ. The given name thereby becomes the Christian name. It is the name by which a person is known to God. For this reason it is the special mark of the members of the community to call one another by their given names. It indicates that they are known personally to one another. It is the familiar (that is, family) way of addressing one another. Children always address one another by the first name, and are so addressed by adults because children are always looked upon with a special concern.

The special relationship that exists among the members of the church is indicated in the common use of the given name at Baptism, for the people of God are united to him and to one another in their faith.

NEIGHBOR In the Old Testament the neighbor is a fellow member of one of the tribes of Israel. All are bound together by the ties of the covenant and law. Each person is required to help the neighbor and is forbidden to harm him.

The New Testament carries the understanding of "neighbor" into a different dimension. Starting from the Old Testament law, "You shall love your neighbor as yourself" (Lev. 19:18), Jesus (in the parable of the good Samaritan) interprets the neighbor as any person who helps one in time of need. The Jews despised the Samaritans as people who disregarded the law, but the Samaritan in the parable was capable of being neighbor to the man who had fallen among thieves. (See Luke 10:25–37.)

The Christian church tried to convey this understanding of the neighbor. They did not confine their deeds of loving-kindness to members of their own community, but sought to help anyone in need, even those who despised and persecuted them. It is true also that the Jewish people had been commanded in the law to remember the stranger and the sojourner. They have always been noted for their support of persons in need anywhere, regardless of religion or nationality. For the Christian, the expression of the love of God that had been shown to them in Jesus Christ was brought forth in their relation to others. It was a form of Christian witness that sometimes puzzled their pagan neighbors, but at the same time impressed them with the quality of the Christian life.

The other side of the story of the good Samaritan is the

obligation to recognize who one's neighbor is. We are to see ourselves in the place of the man in need. The Christian is one who willingly accepts help from whoever offers it, no matter how "different" from himself this neighbor may be.

Christ is the neighbor who helps us. In accepting the neighbor, we recognize the presence of Christ himself. (See Matt. 25:31–46.) In serving the neighbor, we serve Christ.

NEW TESTAMENT   The New Testament is a collection of twenty-seven writings comprising the Christian section of the Bible. "Testament" means "covenant," and the New Testament takes its name from the words of Jesus to his disciples at the Last Supper: "This cup is the new covenant in my blood" (I Cor. 11:25). The Old Testament is the record of God's dealings with his people under the covenant of the law. The New Testament is the record of what God has done in Jesus Christ. It is the sacred writings of the people of the new covenant, the Christian church.

The first Christians knew only one set of Holy Scriptures —the books of the Jewish Bible. But there were circulated in their congregations remembrances of Jesus spoken by those who had known him. There were also letters, particularly those which the apostle Paul wrote to the churches. Some of these remembrances were collected into small "books" as sayings of Jesus or stories about him. They were used for teaching new Christians and informing those who had come to the church seeking to know more about the Christian faith.

As the disciples grew old, the danger of their death under persecution increased. It was realized that the life and work of Jesus Christ needed to be put into a more permanent form. Out of this need there arose the Four Gospels as we have them today. There were other gospels, but these are the four that survived. To them was added The Acts of the Apostles, which is the story of the continuation of the work of Jesus through his church, how the apostles under the power of the Holy Spirit proclaimed the gospel throughout the Roman Empire.

The New Testament continues with a number of letters written to individuals and congregations by Paul and others during the first few decades of the church's life. Doubtless there were other similar letters, but these alone seem to have survived. The final book in the New Testament is called The Revelation to John. It contains messages to seven churches and then continues with a highly dramatic and colorful series of visions that readers have always found puzzling. The Revelation is generally thought to be a symbolic message to churches under persecution, assuring them that although the power of Rome is causing them to suffer, the day will come when God will show himself victorious and they will dwell with him in everlasting joy. (See APOCALYPSE.)

Many writings were held in esteem by the churches, but by the beginning of the fourth century the twenty-seven writings that make up the New Testament as we know it were accepted by most of the churches. One criterion of selection was an intent to preserve the writings that came from the earliest days of the church. Another was to keep the tradition that came from the original apostles and Paul, either directly from their hand or from their remembrances. It is interesting to compare the New Testament writings with the rejected apocryphal writings (see APOCRYPHA). The apocryphal gospels, for example, exhibit less regard for historical accuracy and a greater tendency to preserve wonder stories. Some of the epistles and teaching materials in the apocryphal writings are excellent, but they give a picture of the church as late as the second century.

The intent of the New Testament is to show God's redeeming work among men in Jesus Christ and in the life of the early Christian church. Thus the reading from the New Testament has been a part of the worship of the church; the teaching of the New Testament is a part of education in the church; the preaching of the New Testament message is a part of the mission of the church.

See BIBLE.

O

OBEDIENCE   Obedience is the willingness to do that which we know we must do, on the basis of a recognized authority.

Since people live in groups (family, school, community, church, etc.), it is obvious that if everyone did exactly as he wanted, there would be chaos. Every group of persons needs to have some agreed-upon pattern of living, some accepted behavior; otherwise, there would be only the rule of every person for himself. No one would honor the rights and privileges of others.

For the most part, the lines of authority in our society are fairly well described. In a school there must be some directing head, a principal or headmaster. In any organization of students within the school there must be a central committee, board, or council with responsibility for carrying out the wishes of the organization's members. Such a body also has to have a president or chairman. In the home the parents are responsible for bringing up the children. They must exercise authority while the children are growing into maturity. The children in turn must exercise this responsibility when they establish homes.

Obedience, then, is response to authority in terms of doing what one is asked or expected to do within one's capacity. When those in authority exercise cruelty or demand obedience that creates unnecessary hardship, individuals and/or groups have the right to protest and even to resist the authority. That is their privilege only when injustice is involved. One reason for having courts of law is to decide the rights of individuals and groups who consider themselves to be mistreated or harmed.

Disobedience to rightful authority is sometimes due to the fact that persons are selfish and prideful. In such cases rebelliousness may deserve and receive punishment.

Our religion recognizes God as the only final authority. If

the issues are clear and if obeying man means that the Christian would have to violate his duty to God, he has to make a choice. His duty, then, is to obey God rather than man. Christianity views obedience not so much as an act of fearful duty but as a joyous willingness to be and to do what God expects and desires of his children. So it should be also in our relationships with others. Paul said that husbands and wives, masters and servants, should show love and concern toward one another. (See Eph. 5:21–33; 6:1–9.) When that happens, the authority is exercised in love and so is the obedience. Those in authority do not then exercise this authority to show power but in order to bring out the best that is in those who are responsible to them. The child, the employee, the student, the church member, respond in faithful obedience to those whom they honor and trust in return, knowing that they need not fear or cringe before those who exercise authority in love.

See AUTHORITY; DISCIPLINE.

OFFERING The worship services of the church almost always include the receiving of an offering. Sometimes this is called the "collection," meaning the gathering of funds used for the support of the local church and benevolences (mission work). A concern for the support of the church's work and its ministry to human beings, whether in the church or not, has been characteristic of the church from the beginning.

The word "collection" is not so accurate as is "offering" to describe what should happen when giving takes place within the church. "Offering" means giving to God rather than simply supporting a program. It is out of life that one gives, and that can mean time, energy, self, as well as money. How a person regards material possessions is symbolized by the attitude with which he gives money. It is not so much given to the church as to God, asking his blessing on the gift, the givers, and those who will benefit by the gift. "Offering" implies a giving to God for his glory rather than a showing forth of the willingness to give, or generosity, or even the merits of the program being supported by the gifts. Jesus said that the poor widow who gave her last two coins put in more than those, better off, who put in large sums. "For they all contributed out of their abundance; but she out of her poverty has put in everything she had, her whole living." (Mark 12:41–44.)

True offering, then, will always be seen as a giving of the self (and from the self, the means) to the glory of God. This is the practice of Christian stewardship. (See STEWARDSHIP.) A person is even called upon to give sacrificially; that is, to give up something he might very much want, in order to honor God and further the church's work among men. In doing so, he shows forth in small measure a love for Christ, who gave his very life for man.

In the early church it was customary for people to bring bread and wine which would be offered at the altar, and actually used in the service of the Lord's Supper. They would also bring offerings of food and money which were used for the relief of the poor and others in need. Paul urged the people of the church in Corinth to gather funds for the relief of Christians in Jerusalem: "On the first day of every week [that is, Sunday], each of you is to put something aside and store it up, as he may prosper. . . . And when I arrive, I will send those whom you accredit by letter to carry your gift to Jerusalem" (I Cor. 16:2–3).

The offerings in the church are collected from each individual, and presented before God all together, thus symbolizing the common task to which all are called. Each one's gift combined with the gifts of others makes possible a corporate ministry of service. It is proper that these gifts should be received at the altar and dedicated with prayer to the service of God. The Doxology ("Praise God from whom all blessings flow") is a high point in the service of worship. In the offering the Christian community remembers "the words of the Lord Jesus, how he said, 'It is more blessed to give than to receive'" (Acts 20:35).

See LITURGY; WORSHIP.

OLD TESTAMENT The Bible contains two sections: the Old Testament and the New Testament. These sections were so named by the early Christian church at the time when leaders were deciding what writings they would include permanently in the canon (authorized contents) of the Scriptures. The term "Old Testament" would have had no meaning until after the church had gathered the writings dealing with the life and work of Jesus, and the letters of the apostles, for the first Christians had only the sacred writings that they shared with the Jews. The Old Testament (or Old Covenant) was called by that name because the Christians differentiated between God's covenant with Israel and the new covenant he had now made with the world in Jesus Christ.

The official list of writings to be included in the Old Testament (the Jewish Bible) was not determined until about the second century A.D. Other writings highly regarded were not included in the Old Testament proper but were gathered together in what were called the Apocrypha. (See APOCRYPHA.)

The Old Testament writings cover the events of many thousands of years, and actually were in process of being written and revised over a period of two thousand years. The oldest parts include some early poetry such as the Song of Deborah (Judg., ch. 5). On the other hand, The Book of Daniel was written only a century or so before Christ. Many of the Old Testament books include materials that had been told by word of mouth (the oral tradition) for centuries before they were ever written down. Some of the writings contain materials edited long after the original documents were written.

The Jews divided the books of their Bible into three groups: the Law, the Writings, and the Prophets (the Former and the Latter). The first five books (Genesis through Deuteronomy), containing the law of Moses, were highly regarded.

The Old Testament contains a great variety of types of literature. There are folklore (as in Genesis), history (as in the books of Kings and Chronicles), drama (as in Job), poetry (as in The Song of Solomon), material used in worship (as in The Psalms), preaching (as in many of the prophetic writings), stories (as in Esther and Jonah), pithy sayings (as in The Proverbs). It is a collection of writings in which both Jew and Christian find the written record of the word of God. They will always turn to the Old Testament for spiritual guidance as well as for sheer pleasure in reading.

The Old Testament is important for Christians to know. Some persons in the early church said that since Jesus had come, Christians no longer had to be bound by the Old Testament. The mainstream of the church rejected that idea. It has always been insisted that the gospel of Jesus Christ can be fully understood only when we see it against the background of God's revelation to the people of Israel.

See BIBLE.

ORDINANCE An ordinance is a decree, or law, set forth by one who has the authority to make certain demands. Often in times past kings were thought to have such authority. Laws passed by parliaments were usually called statutes. When a ruler personally made a pronouncement, without the consent of parliament, his decree was called an ordinance.

In theology, however, this word has two meanings. The first has to do with God's own laws, which he and no other could establish. The Jews regarded the law of Moses as an ordinance, in this sense. God gave the law to the people. What he had established was regarded as binding on all Israel. Other laws were created by men and could be changed from time to time. God's decree was not made by any man and therefore could not be changed by man.

The word "ordinance" also has been used sometimes to refer to the rites of the church. Some church bodies refer to the Lord's Supper and Baptism as ordinances rather than as sacraments. In either case, regardless of the designation, these are regarded as having been established by Jesus Christ for the church. Sometimes "sacraments and ordinances" are referred to, meaning by "ordinances" rites such as marriage, confirmation, and ordination, which though recognized by the church as of divine purpose, are not regarded as on the same level with the two sacraments directly commanded by Christ, and which are usually referred to as "dominical" (commanded by the Lord himself).

See LAW; SACRAMENT.

ORDINATION Those called or appointed to leadership in the religious community have usually been set apart to their office by some special rite or ceremony. Among the ancient Hebrews such rites were performed for the priests. The details of the consecration of Aaron and his sons are related in Lev., ch. 8.

The Christian church remembered that Jesus had called the Twelve to share his ministry and carry it on after his death. From the time of the apostles, it was customary to set apart those called to the ministry by a ceremony called the "laying on of hands" (see LAYING ON OF HANDS). The authority to ordain men to this office was usually exercised by the chief pastor in a region, who gradually came to be called a bishop (see BISHOP). It was only the bishops who ordained clergy until the time of the Reformation. At that time those church bodies which gave up the office of bishop continued the practice of ordination, now vested in the regional presbytery or synod or local congregation.

The question of who has the authority to ordain has remained one of the points on which Christian churches are divided. Some churches insist that the ministry is properly thought of only in terms of ordination by bishops who are in the direct line of descent from the original apostles. Other bodies insist that since the church as a whole possesses the authority of Christ, the church may ordain in whatever manner an individual denomination of Christians may prefer. Some say that the person ordained has a different status in the church, since generally only the ordained clergy administer the sacraments and preach. Others view ordination as commissioning a layman for full-time service in the church, regarding him as no different from other laymen except for the special tasks to which he is appointed.

See DEACON; MINISTRY; PRESBYTER.

ORIGINAL SIN   "Original sin" is a term used to describe and to account for man's actual situation in relation to God.

In creating man, God desired to have man respond to him always in perfect love and trust. However, since man could not have been able to show love and trust to God unless he had also the power of choice, God gave man freedom of will.

The story in Gen., ch. 3, of Adam and Eve's choosing to eat fruit (it does not say "apple"!) of the tree of the knowledge of good and evil tells how man chose to follow his own selfish desires instead of trusting God's promises. Original sin refers to this tendency in man to assert his will against God instead of toward or for God.

Although made in the image of God, mankind has spoiled that image by forgetting God and serving self instead of his Maker. Sin consists in claiming self-sufficiency for life instead of acknowledging that all man is and has is a gift from God.

Because man is so deeply infected with this tendency to sin, it is impossible on his own steam, as it were, to do anything to overcome it. But the New Testament affirms that what man cannot do for himself, God does for man. He sends Jesus Christ into the world as perfectly at one with God. By being united to Christ, man's original sin is overcome. Man can become again what he was originally intended to be: restored to the image of God.

See CREATION; REDEMPTION; SIN.

ORTHODOX   Sometimes the word "orthodox" is used to describe accepted standards of belief and practice within the church. In this sense it is opposed to "heretical" (see

HERESY). That is orthodox which conforms to a creed or statement of faith as these are set forth or understood by a particular denomination. For example, in the early nineteenth-century Congregational churches in New England, some leaders objected to the traditional Trinitarian ways of stating Christian doctrine. The newer views were called "unitarian," whereas the traditional Trinitarian views continued to be regarded as "orthodox." A similar thing had happened in the early church. The councils of the church during the first few centuries were called largely to define what were the orthodox, or acceptable, views as over against the heretical views that had come to be popular within certain sections of the church.

A second important use of the term "orthodox" is in connection with the group of churches usually called the Eastern Orthodox Churches. There always had been considerable difference between the churches centered around Rome and those centered around Eastern cities such as Jerusalem, Antioch, Alexandria, and Constantinople. Some of the differences had to do with belief and church practices. The Eastern Churches also did not recognize the bishop of Rome as the chief bishop with authority over them. They preferred to have their churches governed by regional archbishops known as patriarchs. There are many Orthodox Churches, such as the Greek, Russian, Serbian, Bulgarian, and Syrian (India). These churches followed their people to other lands during various migrations. Thus there are many Eastern Orthodox parishes in the United States, Canada, and elsewhere throughout the world.

The Orthodox Churches use the language of the people in their services. Their beliefs are based on the first seven ecumenical councils of the church. One characteristic part of their devotional life is the use of icons (holy pictures), many of which are beautifully painted. Some ceremonies of the Orthodox Churches date back to the earliest centuries. Many of these churches are active members of the World Council of Churches.

P

PARABLE   A parable is a short, pithy statement that sets forth some spiritual meaning. Sometimes it is a very short story. Sometimes it is merely one sentence making a comparison, such as: "The kingdom of heaven is like leaven which a woman took and hid in three measures of meal, till it was all leavened" (Matt. 13:33).

Jesus used the parable as a teaching device. His parables were remembered because they were originally told so vividly that they made a lasting impression and then were passed on by word of mouth.

Jesus drew from the everyday experiences and common problems of his day. To take an example, he told of a Pharisee and a publican who went into the Temple to pray. The Pharisee belonged to a very devout group. Because the Pharisee was proud of being religious, Jesus said, his prayer was of less value than that of the humble publican, who made no pretensions but confessed himself to be a sinner when he came into God's presence. The story gets added point when it is realized that the Pharisees were regarded as a very "proper" religious group, whereas publicans (tax collectors) were detested by most Jews, since they represented the Roman Government, which made the people pay taxes against their will. (See Luke 18:9–14.) Or take the parable of the good Samaritan. Samaritans were looked down upon by Jews of that time because they were people who did not seriously keep the law. The point in the parable is that it was a Samaritan who showed mercy to the man who had been robbed and beaten by thieves. (See Luke 10:25–37.)

It is possible that Jesus sometimes used parables in order to give his disciples a kind of "secret" teaching. There were some matters about the nature of the Kingdom of God that only those who had faith toward God could understand. Those who already understood his teaching would understand its spiritual meaning. Others might hear only the parable. Often Jesus would say, "Let those who have ears hear."

The parables are mostly found in the Gospels of Matthew and Luke. In most cases the exact occasion on which Jesus first used the parable is not known. The Gospel writers often attach the parables they had received by word of mouth to incidents connected with Jesus' ministry.

PARDON The Bible has been called a love story in that it tells of the love of God for man. Sometimes men are shown responding to God's love. Sometimes they disobey God, rejecting him and his promises. Whenever they reject God but later repent, they are welcomed back into the love of God. In one of Jesus' parables a son received from his father a share of the father's estate. Leaving home he squandered all that his father had given him. Finally, he went back home in desperation, only to find that already the father was coming out to greet him, forgiving him his wrongdoing and restoring him to full participation in the life of the family. This is often called the parable of the prodigal son. It is really a story of the forgiving Father. (See Luke 15:11–32.)

Whenever a person is truly sorry (contrite) for his sins, confesses his wrongdoing and wrong attitudes or selfish actions, he is forgiven by God. God grants pardon. In the Lord's Prayer we are taught to pray, "Forgive us our debts, as we forgive our debtors." If God treats us lovingly, granting us his pardon, so ought we to be forgiving toward those who wrongfully treat us.

Sometimes God's pardon is called remission of sins. The sins cannot be denied or erased, for they were committed. But the truly contrite are given a clean slate, as it were. Before one can be fully pardoned, one must seek to repair the wrong done to others or to oneself.

In services of worship some provision is usually made for the confession of sins. The congregation as a whole unites in such a confession. Thus the community of the church as a whole asks God's forgiveness, as well as individuals within the community. The minister usually pronounces a statement that God forgives the sins of those who truly repent. In some churches this is called absolution. The ordained minister of Christ is regarded as having authority to absolve the sins of those who are penitent. "If you forgive the sins of any, they are forgiven; if you retain the sins of any, they are retained." (John 20:23.) These words are recorded as spoken by the risen Lord to the apostles.

Aural confession is confession of sin in the presence of a priest or minister, as in the Roman Catholic Church. The view is that the ordained priest has authority to grant absolution, though the pardon is granted by God alone. The mere confession of sin is no guarantee of pardon. The person seeking forgiveness must be truly sorry for his sin and intend from that time on to be faithful to God's purposes for his life.

See CONFESSION; SIN.

PASSION   The word "Passion" comes from the Latin *passus est,* which implies "suffer" in the old sense of "permit." The term refers to Jesus' obedience to God in his willingness to suffer death on the cross, to allow himself to be used as an instrument in God's purpose for the redemption of mankind. The stirring events leading to Jesus' death so deeply impressed the writers of the Gospels that a great deal of their material refers to the last week of his life on earth.

The events of the Passion are especially commemorated in the church during Holy Week. However, the fifth Sunday in Lent (the Sunday before Palm Sunday) is observed as Passion Sunday in the calendar of the Christian year. In churches of the Catholic tradition, on Passion Sunday the altar cross is covered with a violet veil, which is not removed until Good Friday. This is said to symbolize the withdrawal of Jesus from open preaching and teaching during the period just before his entry into Jerusalem and the events of the Last Week. (See John 11:54.)

From the fourth century on, it became the custom to read

the Gospel accounts of the Last Week in church services during Holy Week. Sometimes these were chanted by the ministers. Gradually a number of musical settings for the Gospel narratives were developed. "Parts" were assigned to the participants, who would sing the words of Jesus and other characters involved in the events. Some of the great composers have written music based on the Passion narratives, one of the most famous being Johann Sebastian Bach's *The Passion According to Saint Matthew.*

The remembrance of Jesus' suffering on the cross and the events leading up to it reminds Christians that they follow One who not only endured the cross himself but who said to his disciples: "If any man would come after me, let him deny himself and take up his cross and follow me" (Mark 8:34).

PASSOVER During a time of famine a number of Hebrew families had gone to Egypt, where they sought opportunities to make a better living. For many years the Hebrews were pressed into hard labor by the Egyptians, who were engaged in building up their cities. When they could stand their oppression no longer, the people, under the leadership of Moses, finally decided to flee from Egypt. The story of their deliverance is told in Ex., ch. 14. The events leading up to the exodus included the Passover, always remembered by the Jews as the time when their forefathers were spared from death by the intervention of God. When the angel of death killed the firstborn among the Egyptians, they themselves were unharmed.

The form in which the Passover festival was to be commemorated is given in Ex., ch. 12. On this annual festival the Jewish people recall the command of Moses: "You shall observe this rite as an ordinance for you and your sons for ever. And when you come to the land which the Lord will give you, as he has promised, you shall keep this service. And when your children say to you, 'What do you mean by this service?' you shall say, 'It is the sacrifice of the Lord's passover, for he passed over the houses of the people of Israel in Egypt, when he slew the Egyptians but spared our houses'" (vs. 24–27).

Passover (called Pesach in Hebrew) is observed by the Jews as one of the great festivals of the year. On the first evening of the season a special meal called the Seder is held in the homes of the people. Special foods remind them of God's deliverance of their ancestors from Egypt. The father leads the ritual, and there are prayers in which all participate.

The Passover became a great national festival. People would make pilgrimages to Jerusalem for the special Passover observances. The events of Jesus' last week took place during the time he and the apostles were in Jerusalem for the Passover.

Later, linking God's deliverance of Israel from Egypt and Christ's deliverance of all men from bondage to evil and death, Christians came to think of the work of Christ as a sort of new Passover. Paul writes: "Christ, our paschal lamb, has been sacrificed." (I Cor. 5:7.) In the death and resurrection of Jesus Christ, God has acted again, as he had in the first Passover, to deliver his people and bring them into the glorious liberty of the children of God.

PEACE   In Gal. 5:22 peace is listed, along with love, joy, patience, kindness, goodness, etc., as a fruit of the Spirit. In Eph. 4:3, Christians are said to be "eager to maintain the unity of the Spirit in the bond of peace." These are only two examples of the many references to peace in the New Testament.

It is assumed in the New Testament that peace is a by-product of being guided by the Holy Spirit. Men do not set out to know the meaning of peace as something they can acquire by their own efforts. Only those who are willing to open themselves to God's direction of their lives discover peace.

Peace is not so much the absence of tension as an attitude toward the tensions that life produces for everybody. It is the recognition that the outcome of all things is in God's hands rather than in our own. We are called to do our best to live calmly in the midst of a world that produces many conflicts. When we are involved in conflicts having to do with right against wrong, standing for the right may cause us hardship and misunderstanding. But those who take part in the struggles of life on God's side will be sustained by the peace of God.

The church is also concerned with peace in a different sense. Members of some bodies of Christians have chosen to be pacifists, opposing war in every case and refusing to bear arms (Friends, Mennonites). Such groups pour their efforts into activities aimed at reducing threats to peace in the world and ministering to all in need regardless of national location. Sometimes other Christians have felt obliged to participate in war as the lesser of evils in cases of the oppression of innocent peoples. However, the church as a whole has always recognized that its mission is to further peace and goodwill among men and that it should work for better understanding among peoples so as to reduce the possibility of war. The church also has stepped in to alleviate the misery that war always produces.

PENTECOST Pentecost was originally a Jewish festival. The word itself comes from the Greek, meaning "the fiftieth day." On the fiftieth day after Passover, it was customary to present the firstfruits of the corn harvest as sacrifices to God. Pentecost, which lasted seven weeks, was a time of rejoicing that God had given the harvest of the crops. "You shall count seven weeks; begin to count the seven weeks from the time you first put the sickle to the standing grain. Then you shall keep the feast of weeks to the Lord your God with the tribute of a freewill offering from your hand, which you shall give as the Lord your God blesses you; and you shall rejoice before the Lord your God." (Deut. 16:9–11.) Later this day also became a time for remembering the giving of the law to Moses.

It was on the Day of Pentecost that the Christian disciples were gathered in Jerusalem, fifty days after Easter. On that occasion they became conscious of the gift of the Holy Spirit. From that time forward they were filled with power to go out into the world, proclaiming the Christian gospel widely and constantly. In fact, the preaching of the gospel began on that very occasion with Peter's sermon to those outside the group of disciples who were curious as to why the Christians were so excited. He explained how God had now fulfilled the promise made through Jesus Christ to send the Holy Spirit. His preaching that day was so moving, we are told, that about three thousand persons were baptized into membership in the church. (See Acts 2:1–42.)

In the course of time, Pentecost became one of the annual festivals, second in importance only to Easter itself as a time for baptism. Because the candidates for baptism wore white garments, the day came to be known also as Whitsunday.

PERFECTION   In Matt. 5:43–48 there is a section of the Sermon on the Mount in which Jesus says that love should be given not only to those who love us, but to all. "Love your enemies and pray for those who persecute you." This section ends with the words, "You, therefore, must be perfect, as your heavenly Father is perfect."

This call to his disciples to be "perfect" refers to perfection in love. His people should seek to let his perfect love enter into their lives so that they, too, shall love their fellowmen as God loves all.

Sometimes people have mistakenly taken this to mean that Jesus is telling them they can be perfect. Because men are created beings, they cannot be perfect. They cannot love perfectly. But when the disciple receives the gift of God's Kingdom, the love of God, which *is* perfect, will show through the disciple's life in his relationships with others.

Sometimes perfection has been held up as a goal for human life. This is usually a mistaken hope. People used to dream of Utopia, some distant day when the world would be so perfectly organized that there would be a kind of perfect society on earth. Many difficult experiences in the modern world, such as the global wars of the twentieth century, have exploded the idea that men could march forward every year making progress toward a perfect world.

Nevertheless, the Christian is called upon to live in the world as a witness to the love of one who is perfect. In doing so, he becomes himself a channel through which light can shine in the darkness. Also the church, when it is true to its Master's commission, shows forth the perfect love of God, even though as an organized institution within the world, made up of imperfect persons, it cannot itself be perfect.

In other words, perfection belongs to God alone. The day in which the world is perfected must always await the intention of God alone. Christians must never forget that in their imperfect lives they seek to follow the only One who ever showed forth perfect love on earth.

See LOVE.

PETITION   Petition is one of the ingredients of prayer. It means, literally, "an asking."

In petition one lays before God some need or problem concerning which his guidance and help are desired. Because people are incomplete and helpless in many situations, they turn in faith to the only one who can help them. Petition springs from the sense of aloneness in individual need.

Sometimes people say, "Why should we bother God with our little needs?" Actually, God as the loving Heavenly Father is concerned about the whole of life; nothing is too little or unimportant for him to be too busy to heed. As people grow in spiritual understanding, however, they find themselves asking God's help chiefly with regard to the major problems and needs of life. God is not a celestial Santa Claus, writing down lists of things people ask for and giving them out as requested. Rather, he is to be thought of as desiring deeper and better life for his people than they themselves could imagine. Sometimes a person asks selfishly or ignorantly. God will forgive such presumption, but he will not answer prayers simply because they are made. The prayer of Jesus in Gethsemane becomes a model at this point. He prayed, in the face of the coming crucifixion, "My Father, if it be possible, let this cup pass from me." But he concludes his petition, having perfect faith in God's will for him as the only thing that really mattered, "Nevertheless, not as I will, but as thou wilt" (Matt. 26:39).

It has been argued that one should ask God only for "spiritual" help. God is interested in the whole self, and not just in the so-called "spiritual" life. In the Lord's Prayer one says, "Give us this day our daily bread." Food is a material need of all. It is right to infer that no matter what the need —physical, mental, or spiritual—it is perfectly proper to lay anything before God. However, one should not think that by asking, one will always get what one wants. Wants and real needs may often be two quite different matters.

PRAYER   Prayer is the means through which man communicates with God. All religions, whether primitive or modern, seem to have some sort of prayer. In primitive religions, prayer is often akin to magic: an attempt, through properly expressed liturgy and sacrifices, to appease a god, win his favor, and be granted a desire.

The kind of prayer used by a religious group reflects its understanding of the god it worships. The Christian understanding of prayer comes from its use in the Bible, beginning with the Old Testament. Here were people who believed that there was one God above all the gods to whom men prayed. Eventually they came to believe that he alone was God and those whom others worshiped were merely inventions of their imaginations. They were a whole people, and the prayer they offered to God was made in behalf of the group rather than of any individual. They were sure that God led them as a people, rewarded them as a people, and punished them as a people.

Later books of the Old Testament indicate a gradual awareness of God's concern for each person as an individual and the consequent development of personal devotion. Although many of the psalms are prayers for use in public worship, some of them are deep expressions of individual need. It is noteworthy that the people of the Bible never prayed from a sense of fear, hoping to appease a God whose ways they could not understand. They always prayed to a God in whom they had sure confidence. Since all his ways were wise and all his purposes good, there was no need to try to force his decisions by magic rites. Theirs was not a God far off, but one near at hand.

The Temple at Jerusalem saw one form of prayer, centering around the sacrifices and the great festivals to which the people came from afar. The synagogue in each village, where people attended the Sabbath services each week, saw another form of corporate prayer by the congregation and their lay leaders. The personal religious life in the family centered around the observance of personal devotion three times a day, thanksgiving before meals, and a special blessing in the home at the beginning and close of the Sabbath.

The disciples of Jesus would have continued the forms of prayer already familiar to them. The Gospels record that Jesus himself went alone to pray on more than one occasion, and they evidently knew where to find him. After a busy Sabbath Day in Capernaum, it is written, "And in the morning, a great while before day, he rose and went out to a lonely place, and there he prayed" (Mark 1:35).

To the Christian, God is a Person (that is, a living, active Presence). He can be known only as one has contact with him. Prayer is talking with God. Thoughts are put before God in words. He does not reply in words, but by his Holy Spirit he seeks his people even as they turn toward him.

It may be said that the basic form of prayer is petition, for a person will reveal his need and ask for help only from one whom he loves and trusts. (See PETITION.) Intercession is a similar form of prayer, for it is petition for others. (See

INTERCESSION.) Jesus at another time told his disciples that it was useless for them to expect God to forgive their sins if they did not forgive those who had hurt them (Matt. 6:14–15). This suggests that confession is another form of prayer. (See CONFESSION.)

There are forms of prayer in which the person turns from himself and his needs to expressions of awe, wonder, and gratitude in the presence of the Holy God. Adoration is this kind of prayer, in which one bows in God's presence, honoring him for his own sake and acknowledging him as Creator and Sustainer of all that is, the Almighty Ruler of heaven and earth. Thanksgiving is another form of prayer. Men have received from God more than they could ever need. He has made provision for their physical needs; he gives them minds with which to think, the capacity to feel deeply and to know right from wrong. He has surrounded them with friends, opportunities, and joys. Even difficulties, sorrows, and disappointments often turn out in the end to have been blessings when they can be seen in perspective. God the Heavenly Father is to be thanked for these and all other mercies.

Through this relationship to God in prayer, persons are enabled to receive his love and to live according to his purposes. Through his Holy Spirit he comes to men and helps them to come to him.

PRESBYTER The first Christians found it necessary to have certain officers who would be responsible for different aspects of the life of the church.

One of these officers, or leaders, was called the presbyter (or elder). In the Jewish synagogues the government of the community was in charge of officers called elders. The term was taken over by the church. We read of their work in passages such as Acts 11:30 and Acts 15:22. In Acts 14:23 we are told how Paul and Barnabas appointed elders for some of the churches that they had helped to get started. These presbyters (elders) functioned as overseers and ministers.

In two of the later New Testament writings we see how their work developed. In James 5:14 there is a reference to the presbyters' care of the sick through prayer and anointing. In I Peter 5:1–4 advice is given to the presbyters: "So I exhort the elders among you . . . Tend the flock that is your charge, not by constraint but willingly, not for shameful gain but eagerly, not as domineering over those in your charge but being examples to the flock. And when the chief Shepherd is manifested you will obtain the unfading crown of glory."

By the second century the term "bishop" is used for those who have been selected as presidents of groups of presbyters. In time the ministerial leaders of the church seem to have divided into bishops (the chief presbyters), presbyters (elders), and deacons. The English word "priest" (used by some churches today) has the same Greek origin as the word "presbyter." The two words really have the same meaning. (See Bishop; Deacon; Ministry.)

In churches of the Reformed (Presbyterian) tradition the term "elder" refers either to the teaching elder, who is an ordained minister, or to the ruling elder, a layman ordained to serve on the governing board of his local church. In The Methodist Church the fully ordained minister is called elder.

See Ordination.

PRIDE Pride is thinking of ourselves more highly than we ought to think. It is putting self in the center rather than giving recognition to God as the true center of life. Pride has been called the principal sin of man, because from it spring all sorts of other sinful attitudes and actions. If *we* take the center of the stage, we are so much wrapped up in ourselves that we cannot see our weaknesses, shortcomings, and wrongdoing.

Pride takes many forms. In some persons it is concentration on satisfying their own needs even at the expense of the consideration due to others. In some it is a feeling of superiority of oneself to other persons, or of one's group or race to other groups and races. Sometimes it is purely personal, as when an individual shows haughty attitudes toward someone he considers beneath himself in appearance, social standing, or education. Sometimes a kind of pride is shared with large numbers of others. Collectively their pride can become the source of hatred toward large masses of people. Nations, for example, as well as individuals, can be overly proud.

What happens to people who succumb to pride? They eventually cut themselves off from true relationships with other persons. They introduce snobbery and prejudice into the world. They divorce themselves from God. Pride puts the self in place of God. The Bible warns against the fruits of pride:

"Pride goes before destruction,
　　and a haughty spirit before a fall.
　It is better to be of a lowly spirit with the poor
　　than to divide the spoil with the proud."
(Prov. 16:18–19.)

Again, the Bible predicts that human pride will always come to nothing in the end:

"And the haughtiness of man shall be humbled,
　　and the pride of men shall be brought low;
　　and the Lord alone will be exalted in that day."
(Isa. 2:17.)

Jesus said, "Blessed are the meek, for they shall inherit the earth." (Matt. 5:5.)

It should be noted also that sometimes religious people can be overly proud of their very religion itself. Jesus condemned certain persons who in their pride felt they were better than others. It is even possible for very humble persons to be proud of their humility. However, a truly humble person is one who knows his limitations before God, yet has strength of character and purpose. He recognizes that God calls him to make a contribution in terms of his God-given talents and personhood.

See SIN.

PROCLAMATION To proclaim something is to announce in no uncertain tones what is true or accomplished. For example, Presidential proclamations are statements coming directly from the hand of the Chief Executive of the nation. These must be taken seriously by all citizens, for they contain messages of sufficient importance for the head of the nation to state them for the public information and welfare.

The word "proclamation" refers to that which is announced. In the New Testament the word is used in two ways: heralding that which is to come (as John the Baptist announced that the Messiah was about to come); announcing that which already has happened (the fact that Jesus Christ has come from God to bring salvation to mankind, which the Gospel writers proclaimed).

The gospel was proclaimed to those who had not yet heard the good news about Christ. The apostles, the first preachers of the church, went into the village market places and city squares to tell those who gathered around them that God had visited and redeemed his people. They invited those who heard to believe the good news, repent of their sins, receive the forgiveness of God and the gift of the Holy Spirit, and be baptized.

How do we know what the proclamation of the early church was? It can be found in the preaching of Peter, as recorded in The Acts of the Apostles. Peter referred to the words of the prophet Joel, who foretold a time when the will of God would be fulfilled. Then he announced that this had happened in the life and death of Jesus Christ, whom God had raised from the dead. Jesus, whom his enemies had sought to destroy, had returned by his Holy Spirit to be with the church. Someday he would return in glory.

When the minister stands in the pulpit to preach a sermon he continues to proclaim the gospel. However, there is a difference between proclaiming the gospel to those who do not yet believe and to those who already are believers. Those who are members of the church need to be reminded of the gospel and taught what it means for their daily living.

Preaching *in* the church usually is intended for the upbuilding of the people in the gospel, which they have already heard, and to which they have responded in their Baptism.

PROPHECY Among the Hebrews certain individuals from time to time were thought to have special talents for interpreting the meanings of various happenings. If individuals or the community as a whole wanted to know the significance of some unclear event, they would seek out a seer. These seers were regarded highly by the leaders of the people as well as by the populace in general. They were thought to possess insights and powers greater than those of ordinary folk.

In the course of time the people tended to turn to the priests attached to shrines and holy places when such interpretations were sought. Sometimes there was rivalry between the independent seers and the regular priesthood. There also arose a group of persons not necessarily either seers or priests who pondered God's requirements for the people. These men, called prophets, uttered warnings about the punishment and danger that would come to the people when God's demands were ignored.

The great prophets were humble persons (Amos, the shepherd) or persons from families of high influence and social standing (Isaiah). Their messages, as we have them recorded in the Bible, were either written down by themselves or remembered by disciples who wrote them down later. The earlier seers had usually been thought of as predicting future happenings. The later prophets took a deep look at current events and stated that in the present situation the will of God was thus and so. "This is what God says" was the prophets' message. In a sense this was still a kind of foretelling, for the prophets warned that if the people did not mend their ways and follow God's will, certain dire results would follow. If they listened to God's will and sought to obey him, peace and blessedness would be assured.

The prophets looked forward to a day when God would

send the Messiah to establish his Kingdom on earth. The Christians were convinced that Jesus Christ was the one whom the prophets had said would come. They recognized through faith that it was indeed Jesus who had fulfilled the purposes of God for the destiny of men.

PROTESTANT   Originally the word "protest" meant "to stand for." Today it usually means "to stand against." The word "Protestant" contains both meanings.

"Protestant" denotes that part of the Western church which broke away from the Roman Catholic Church in the sixteenth century. It was a time of ferment in several directions. A fresh surge of learning had enlarged horizons and brought new insights into the arts and sciences. The English, German, French, and other nations were becoming conscious of their individuality. In the church, many of the higher clergy had become corrupt, while the ignorance of the parish clergy was equally alarming. These were some of the factors that led to the Reformation.

Earlier reform movements had been started by Wycliffe in England, Hus in Bohemia, and Waldo in northern Italy. But the immediate cleavage in the church came as a result of Martin Luther's protest against the sale of indulgences. His formal thesis, meant for scholars, unleashed forces that arose both because the German princes wanted independence from papal (and Italian) rule and because the people were indignant over the grasping after money by the rulers of the church. The revolt spread throughout northern Europe. Calvin's reformation, beginning in Geneva, took hold in Switzerland, France, and Scotland. Pietist groups arose throughout Europe. Through migrations to the new world, Protestantism eventually became the prevailing form of Christianity in the United States and Canada.

Although Protestants share most of the basic Christian understandings in common with the Roman Catholic Church, the points of difference are important enough to have continued the break for five hundred years. Protestantism affirms that man is freed from sin by faith alone. (See JUSTI-FICATION.) Good works will not help; they can only be expressions of gratitude for what God has done. Grace is the free-flowing love of God, which can never be controlled by priestly actions through sacraments. That is, grace is found in the sacraments but not confined to them. (See GRACE.) Man is not made partially able to understand God because he possesses reason, but is completely in need of God's saving grace in order to know God and be released from sin. The Bible contains all things necessary to salvation, and no doctrine can be derived solely from the tradition of the church. The universal priesthood of believers incorporates Luther's affirmation that Christians must constantly inter-cede for one another and be as Christ to one another. The doctrine recognizes that the church is God's work but in-sists that it shares the gift of freedom given to all men, and that it too can sin and fail to fulfill God's purposes for its life.

Protestantism includes many denominations, some widely divergent from others. There are closely ordered commun-ions and "free" churches in which the local church is an autonomous (or nearly so) unit. There are varieties of Biblical and theological interpretations and forms of wor-ship. Today the stress is on similarities, and an ecumenical approach is bringing the larger groups into closer relation-ships. Indeed, there are even the beginnings of friendly conversations looking toward mutual understandings with the Roman Catholic Church.

PROVIDENCE   The word "providence" contains a smaller word, "provide." This is the key to its meaning. Providence refers to the work of God the Provider. God created the world and all that lives in it, but this was not the end of his work. He did not withdraw from his world, leaving it to take care of itself. The Bible shows a God who is always working in the world and always concerned with his creatures. He provides for their needs. Jesus pointed this out when he said: "Consider the lilies, how they grow; they neither toil nor spin; yet I tell you, even Solomon in all his glory was not arrayed like one of these. But if God so clothes the grass which is alive in the field today and tomorrow is thrown into the oven, how much more will he clothe you, O men of little faith!" (Luke 12:27–28). If God clothes the lilies of the field and feeds the birds of the air, he will most surely also clothe and feed his human children.

This must not be taken to mean that God will give people whatever they wish. It means only that they can trust him not to desert them in their need.

The providential work of God extends to all the needs of his people. When people are sick, they know that God will sustain them; when they are in trouble, they know that he will help them; when they are dying, they know that he will be with them as they enter more fully into eternal life. He provides for them as they have faith that he will do so, as they trust in him. They are able to do this because they know from the Old and New Testaments that he has provided for his people.

The providential work of God is seen also in the history of nations, in the rise and fall of governments, in the destruction or fulfillment of cultures. God is holy, and his purposes are fulfilled in spite of, as well as through, the works of men. Sometimes his purpose is fulfilled through suffering rather than through escape from suffering. This is summed up in the apostle Paul's experience: "We know that in everything God works for good with those who love him" (Rom. 8:28).

Providence does not mean that life will always be happy, the weather sunny, and that events will run smoothly. It means that God is ruler of the world he has made, that his purposes will be fulfilled in his own time, and that those who love and trust him will be sustained in every need.

PURGATORY Purgatory was thought to be the place of departed spirits. This belief arose during the Middle Ages in answer to the question, How can sinful man enter into the perfection of God's presence? To be sure, the Christian was one who had been redeemed by Christ and forgiven his sin, but even at the end of a good life he was far from being what God desired him to be and needed still more time to achieve that goal. (See PERFECTION.)

The question was answered by belief in an intermediate place or state between earthly existence and heaven. This was not thought of as a place of never-ending suffering, as was hell. The suffering of purgatory had as its purpose to cleanse the soul of earthly affections, earth-bound ways, and the imperfections of human existence. How long a person stayed in purgatory depended on his need for preparation to become worthy of life with God.

This belief became a major concern for people. It was thought that every deed—good and bad—was balanced in the record of a life. Naturally, one wanted to make the record as good as possible in order to reduce the time of suffering. The church helped people feel they were reaching that goal in a specific way by saying that if a person attended certain services, made pilgrimages, and gave offerings, he was subtracting from the total time in purgatory. A system of "indulgences" developed by which a person, by giving certain amounts of money, could cut down the time that a loved one, already dead, would have to spend in purgatory. But no one was ever really sure what the penalties were or how they could be decreased.

The selling of indulgences reached a point where it became a contributory cause of the Protestant Reformation. Martin Luther protested that the grace of God could not be measured and the mercy of God could not be bought. It has been basic in Protestantism to reject the doctrine of purgatory. Admitting that no one is really worthy to enter the holy presence of God, nevertheless the Christian believes that he is brought there clothed in the righteousness of Christ his Lord. He believes that if the saving work of Christ means anything, it means that he is saved from the wages of sin, which is death, and given eternal life, now as well as forever. (See Rom. 6:23.)

The doctrine of purgatory is given its Biblical basis in I Peter 3:18–20; 4:6, where Christ is said to have visited the place of departed spirits between his death and resurrection. Whatever this may have meant to the writer of the epistle, Protestants have rejected it as a basis for belief in an intermediary state after death. Roman Catholics, however, take this belief seriously, and it is thought to rest in the justice of God. They hope, through following the requirements of their church concerning this doctrine, to face this purifying suffering and finally to come, sinless, into the presence of God for eternity.

See DEATH; HEAVEN; HELL.

R

RECONCILIATION   It is God's desire that persons should have fellowship with him. Because people are selfish, they set up barriers between themselves and God. They try to "live it alone," following the customs of men, obeying earthly laws but ignoring the commandments of God and forgetting to serve him.

The result is that they become separated from God. They find themselves increasingly unhappy and miserable because aside from their selfish ways they lack purpose for living. It was to people in such a condition that Jesus Christ was sent by God. He continues to come into the world by his Holy Spirit to change lives.

Paul refers to this as the process of reconciliation. When someone follows Christ he becomes a new creature. Old things pass away and all things become new. This is how he puts it: "God was in Christ reconciling the world to himself" (II Cor. 5:19). Through Christ, men are brought into a right relationship with God. The result is that all who follow Christ are called to be "ambassadors for Christ" (v. 20). They will live differently with one another because they are brought by faith into a new relationship with God through Jesus Christ.

In the New Testament it is always God who takes the initiative in bringing sinful men into this new life with him. He does this because of his love for man, even though man does not deserve such love. Those who have been reconciled to God through Christ then become witnesses to the new creation by the way in which they live in the world. They will seek to reconcile enemies, to break down barriers, to build up strong ties of love with all others, because they have had committed to them "the message of reconciliation" (v. 19).

REDEMPTION   If someone gives a possession into the keeping of another person or sells it to him, with the understanding that the ownership has been relinquished, and if after that, decides he wants it back, there are only two ways to repossess it. Either the new owner gives it up voluntarily, restoring it to the original possessor, or else the former owner pays for it in money or services in order to get it back. The process by which this takes place is called "redemption," and the word itself has entered the Christian vocabulary.

In the Old Testament, "redemption" is used in connection with beliefs that date way back to the early days of Israel. It was thought that the firstborn offspring of a man's cattle belonged to God. If the owner desired to keep the animal for some other purpose than sacrifice to God, he would have to provide an acceptable substitute. If a person was sold into slavery, the only way he could gain his freedom was to pay a ransom price or have someone else do that for him.

The idea developed that as the whole people of Israel belonged to God, the only way they could be delivered from their problems and miseries would be by the action of a deliverer or redeemer. A price had to be paid if they were to be freed from slavery in Egypt, if they were to enter the Promised Land, if they were to be restored to their former homeland after exile in Babylon. As a relative might act on behalf of a person who was in serious trouble, paying the price of his release, so God was regarded as having himself paid the price of their deliverance.

In the writing contained in the closing chapters of The Book of Isaiah there are many references to the Servant of God who will be sent to redeem his people Israel from their sorrows and sins. "He was despised and rejected by men; a man of sorrows, and acquainted with grief. . . . Surely he has borne our griefs and carried our sorrows; yet we esteemed him stricken, smitten by God, and afflicted. But he was wounded for our transgressions, he was bruised for our iniquities; upon him was the chastisement that made us whole, and with his stripes we are healed. All we like sheep have gone astray; we have turned every one to his own way; and the Lord has laid on him the iniquity of us all." (Isa. 53:3–6.)

It was in such a frame of reference that the disciples saw Jesus. He was the Son of God who laid down his life for the world. "As the Father knows me, and I know the Father; and I lay down my life for the sheep." It is not for his friends only that he is willing to face the cross: "I have other sheep, that are not of this fold; I must bring them also, and they will heed my voice. So there shall be one flock, one shepherd." (John 10:15–16.) Jesus sheds his blood in order that all who believe in him may be gathered into his faithful community, the church. What the observance of the law could not do to make men right with God has been accomplished in the death of Christ. Because of the redemption that Christ has accomplished, our sins are forgiven, we are brought close to God, and we are united with all other believers to do his will on earth.

Paul refers to our having been "bought with a price"—the sacrifice of Jesus Christ on the cross. (I Cor. 6:20; 7:23.) Therefore we are no longer slaves but sons of God, called to live joyfully, serving our fellowmen in the spirit of Christ and the love of God.

See ATONEMENT; SALVATION.

RELIGION   Wherever a person looks in the world, he finds certain beliefs and practices among every people that can be described only by the word "religion."

One way to describe religion is to think of it as the way in which people are related to what is the most important reality in the world for them, as the English word "religion" implies. It means "that to which one is bound," that to which he gives his fullest loyalty. In this sense it can be said that everyone has a religion, because everyone puts the highest value on some factor in his life.

However, religion is usually recognized as something that involves more than just an individual's center of values. Whole groups of people can be seen to follow a way of life related to what they regard as of most importance. Usually this has to do with the way in which the gods, or God, are thought of and worshiped. Large numbers of people are found to hold approximately the same ideas about God and to follow practices that bind them together in their worship of him. Together they follow some form of contact with the deity. In some cases this god is thought of in national or local terms. In the great world religions he is regarded as being universal—everywhere the same, regardless of where his worshipers may be.

It is thus possible to speak of "a religion"—the distinctive beliefs and practices of a large section of humanity. Some of these religions are chiefly ethical, that is, they are principally concerned with right behavior among people (such as Confucianism). Some, such as Hinduism and most of Buddhism, believe that man should escape from the ties of this life by seeking a union with God that is completely beyond this human existence. Islam, Judaism, and Christianity are called theistic. That is, they affirm a God who is closely related to the world he has made, acting in and through the events of history.

Within all the great world religions there are various interpretations held by different sects, each of which has its own practices. Some religions are highly missionary—seeking to win converts. Others are content to be confined chiefly to their own places of origin (such as Shinto, found mostly in Japan). Sometimes people make the mistake of referring to sects or denominations within a religion as "religion." Hence, if someone asks a Christian, "What is your religion?" the proper reply would be "Christian" rather than Baptist, Presbyterian, Roman Catholic, etc. All denominations within Christianity have much more in common with one another as Christian groups than they have with any other religion.

REMEMBRANCE To remember something is to recall it, to bring it to mind, to focus attention on it. Thus people can remember persons, experiences, ideas, or events. They cannot remember matters that never involved them.

Christians are brought face to face with the personalities and events of Jewish-Christian history. The principal ones are recorded in the Bible. Those who read and study acquire a knowledge that they do not easily lose. They grow familiar with these writings; whenever a name or event is mentioned or encountered in reading, it rings a bell in their minds.

However, there is a deeper meaning in "remembrance." The mere recalling of facts from the Bible or church history, etc., is no different from the recalling of other things that have been learned through study or firsthand experience. Christians remember in a deeper way. Certain persons and events stand out so importantly (if they have really become known from inside the life of the community of faith) that what happened a long time ago becomes part of a living memory in which the Christian participates today.

An example of this is the way in which Christians celebrate the Lord's Supper together. Jesus told his disciples to continue to break bread and drink the cup in remembrance of him. Ever since, when Christians have done this in their churches, the events of the Last Supper with Jesus in the upper room at Jerusalem have come to life. In the very act of remembering, they participate with the disciples and with all the faithful across the generations who have remembered

Christ in this form. The remembrance takes the form of the living presence of Christ with his people rather than being merely a commemoration of something that happened a long time ago.

All the common acts of worship of the church imply this participation in some degree. Remembrance is the process whereby the acts of God for man's salvation are brought to mind in terms of actions that are still of great concern. God did not act only in the past; he acts in the midst of his people today, especially when they relive in their common life the meaning of the great events by which he made himself known to the world in Jesus Christ. Good Friday, for example, brings vividly into memory Jesus' death on the cross, for he died there for us too. Easter is a reminder that God raised Jesus from the dead and that the Spirit of the risen Christ still lives in the world powerfully through the life of the whole church.

REMNANT   The people of Israel are shown in the Bible to have been chosen by God as his very own. Through them he chose to accomplish his purposes for the world. This close relationship of Israel to God is shown in the fact that Israel is called by intimate names: Son, Servant, Bride.

There had never been a time, though, when all the people of Israel were willing to say yes to God's call. Thus many of the prophets developed the idea of the "remnant." This was a smaller group within the whole nation to whom the fruits of the covenant would be reserved. Since God could not count on one hundred percent faithfulness, those who did remain faithful in their worship and faith would be the carriers of his plan of salvation in the world.

An early interpretation of the remnant idea is contained in Gen. 18:23–33. The city of Sodom is about to be destroyed because of the wickedness of the people there. Abraham pleads that God spare the city. God promises to do this if there are even ten righteous people to be found. For their sake he will withhold the destruction of the entire city.

The remnant is also referred to in the latter part of The Book of Isaiah. These chapters were written by a prophet of the exile after the leaders of the people had been carried away to Babylonia in the year 587 B.C. The Temple had been destroyed by the enemy. Israel had fallen because of its sins. This prophet (usually referred to as the Second Isaiah to distinguish him from the earlier Isaiah after whom the book is named) portrays Israel as the Servant of the Lord. It is Israel's task to suffer not only for her own sins but to be "as a covenant to the people, a light to the nations, to open the eyes that are blind, to bring out the prisoners from the dungeon, from the prison those who sit in darkness" (Isa. 42:6–7).

The Christian community identified the Suffering Servant with Christ. As they shared in Christ's death and resurrection they became the New Israel. They thought of themselves as the remnant who would carry on the witness to God's purpose in the world.

Within the church itself at various periods in its history small groups have risen to protest when the church became too self-satisfied. There is always the possibility that if the church at large gets too powerful or not different enough from the world around it, its purest form will be preserved by small groups within its life. Small groups, however, can never be the remnant. They, too, may have a mistaken notion of their own importance. Only God knows to whom he will turn to accomplish his purposes in the world.

REPENTANCE Repentance refers to acknowledging wrong-doing or sin and doing something about it. Just saying one is sorry for a wrong done against God or a fellowman is not enough.

The prophets of the Old Testament talked of the need for Israel to repent. Time and again Israel forgot the covenant God had made with them, preferring to worship pagan gods and doing other things that were displeasing to God. The prophets arose to remind the people that only by repenting and being faithful to the covenant could they be restored to right relationship with God.

John the Baptist preached "a baptism of repentance for the forgiveness of sins" (Mark 1:4). He was preparing the way for Jesus. After his baptism by John, Jesus "came into Galilee, preaching the gospel of God, and saying, 'The time is fulfilled, and the kingdom of God is at hand; repent, and believe in the gospel,'" (Mark 1:14–15).

Repentance means returning to God after a person has forgotten to serve him. It means changing habits, attitudes, and ways of life, wherever necessary, in order to live for God.

Repentance involves decision and commitment—that is, waking up to the fact that something is wrong in the repentant person's relation to God. He decides that he will remember to serve God instead of forgetting and hurting him. The same will be true of his relations with other persons with whom, perhaps, he has fallen out. He comes to the point of knowing that insofar as he was at fault, it is his responsibility to turn around and do something to try to restore good relations. This is not always easy to do. It may mean changing a great deal. But the sincerely penitent person knows that God helps him to live in true commitment to the way of Christ.

See CONTRITION; FORGIVENESS; SIN.

RESURRECTION   Jesus was crucified on the Friday of his last week on earth. The disciples were mournful and distressed. Now their Lord had been taken from them. But on Sunday the joyful word spread among them that he was not in the tomb—he had risen. They remembered his promise, now fulfilled, that he would come to them. He had taught them "that the Son of man must suffer many things, and be rejected by the elders and the chief priests and the scribes, and be killed, and after three days rise again" (Mark 8:31). The Gospels report the experiences of the disciples in meeting the risen Christ. These stories are given in Mark, ch. 16; Luke, ch. 24; Matt., ch. 28; and John, chs. 20 to 21.

The realization that God had raised Jesus from the dead turned the disciples from despair to gladness, from weakness to power. Now they knew that indeed the man they had known in the flesh had been the One anointed of God, and that he would be alive in the world through his church forever.

Reflecting on the resurrection later, Paul wrote: "For I delivered to you as of first importance what I also received, that Christ died for our sins in accordance with the scriptures, that he was buried, that he was raised on the third day in accordance with the scriptures, and that he appeared to Cephas, then to the twelve. Then he appeared to more than five hundred brethren at one time, most of whom are still alive, though some have fallen asleep. Then he appeared to James, then to all the apostles. Last of all, as to one untimely born, he appeared also to me" (I Cor. 15:3–8).

It has always been the central Christian conviction that since God raised Christ from the dead, we can be raised to a new life with him. In Baptism, a man is said to have been buried with Christ and also to be raised with him. Those who belong to him (through the church) are completely identified with him. As it is written elsewhere: "If then you have been raised with Christ, seek the things that are above, where Christ is, seated at the right hand of God." (Col. 3:1.)

See EASTER.

REVELATION How do people know about God? One way might be to look for him, to try to find out all about him through the mind. The planets move around the sun in an ordered course. The navigator can always chart the course of the ship or the airplane by the positions of the stars. The sun "rises" in the east or "sets" in the west. Spring is followed by summer, and fall precedes winter. These and hundreds of other "evidences" point to a design in the universe. One scientist said that the world is so perfectly organized that its designer must be thought of as "the great mathematician." Thus it can be said that since the universe seems to move according to definite patterns, there must be some purpose back of it all. One might say this proves that God is.

However, revelation does not refer to man's search for God but to God's disclosure of himself to man. That means starting from an entirely different point. All that can be known about God is what he chooses to let men know about himself. The word "revelation" is properly used to refer to this self-revelation on the part of God.

Sometimes theologians have talked of "general revelation." By this they mean that God does show something of himself to man in the very ordering of his creation and in the powers of reason that he has given to man. The Bible, however, does not ask the question, How can God be proved to exist? It starts with the assumption that God is, and that he takes the initiative in revealing his nature and his purposes.

In the first place, God reveals himself through his acts. For the Jews, the supreme act of God was his selection of them as the people through whom he would accomplish his purpose in the world. He acted to show himself to them by delivering them from slavery in Egypt (the exodus) and leading them through the wilderness to the Promised Land. He showed himself to them by making a covenant with Moses on Mt. Sinai. God, by his actions, revealed his mercy and loving-kindness as well as his judgment to them.

Christians know God by his action in Jesus Christ, in whom he shows the fullness of his love for men. The revelation of God to his people reaches its climax in a particular Person, Jesus Christ. By taking human flesh upon himself, God completely identifies himself with human needs. Men know him when, by loving obedience to the way of Jesus Christ, they remain faithful to his call. Another way to speak of revelation is to say that he seeks men before they seek him. They do not so much find him as they are found by him.

God reveals himself in history and in Jesus Christ. He also is revealed in the Scriptures. The Bible is the written record of the revelation of God. It is a human book that discloses the whole drama of redemption. Only in the Bible is the history of God's relation to mankind found. The men who wrote the books of the Bible were setting forth their understanding of the meaning of God's revelation. By their testimony, people today can learn of God's revelation when they read these writings in faith.

See BIBLE; NEW TESTAMENT; OLD TESTAMENT.

RIGHTEOUSNESS The term "righteousness" is used in the Bible in two ways. First, it refers to a quality in God. God is righteous, that is, he is always perfectly trustworthy, fair, and merciful in his dealings with the persons he has made. God cannot be false, unjust, or mean, for that would be contrary to his very nature. In fact, God is the only righteous one of whom one could possibly think. If he were not so, he would be less than God. Man could not trust and worship a god whose actions were governed by whim rather than by consistent purpose.

The Hebrews regarded God's righteousness as being disclosed in the law given to Moses. In the covenant with his chosen people, God promised to be with them always. They were to be faithful to God. He would not tolerate playing lightly with the law, for that would be evidence of faithlessness on the part of the people.

The second way in which the term is used is in reference to relations among persons. Righteousness, which comes from God, must also be the spirit in which people should treat one another. However, no man can be perfectly righteous as God is righteous. Men can be righteous only if God makes it possible to be so. Keeping the law, Jesus said, was not enough. There had to be an inner righteousness greater than that of merely keeping the law. It is in sharing with Christ that the meaning of righteousness is learned. Man can be made righteous only by faith. This does not mean that a person becomes perfectly righteous. Only God can be that. But if a man learns through Christ the meaning of the forgiveness of sins by God, he will then be able to live in the light of the righteousness that God shares with all who turn to him. The unrighteous are the godless, those who turn against him.

RITUAL   A ritual is the form used for a service of worship. In some churches the ritual is set by church law. The services always follow the same order, week by week. Usually there is a wide variety of materials, arranged according to the different seasons of the church year. For example, the Old and New Testament lessons change day by day, as do the collects prescribed for each Sunday.

In some churches the ritual is not set in the same ordered pattern. The minister is free to choose materials as he sees fit from any source. However, even when the ritual is a "free" one, a congregation follows approximately the same order of worship each week. Otherwise, they would not know what to expect and there would be confusion in following the service.

Some items appear as part of the ritual of almost every church. One of these is the Lord's Prayer. Another is the use of ancient hymns of the church, such as the Gloria Patri ("Glory be to the Father") and the Doxology ("Praise God from whom all blessings flow"). Scripture passages used as opening sentences (calls to worship) are familiar, such as "The Lord is in his holy temple" (Hab. 2:20); also, the words used at the offertory, such as "Remember the words of the Lord Jesus . . ." (Acts 20:35). The words of Jesus at the Last Supper are almost always used during the service of the Lord's Supper: "Take, eat," etc.; and "Drink this," etc.

Ritual is also provided by most denominations for rites such as Baptism, marriage, burial of the dead, confirmation, or reception of members, and ordination. "Ritual" should not be confused with "ceremony." Ritual refers to the words or form used. Ceremony has to do with the way in which the service is conducted.

See Ceremony; Ordination; Sacrament.

S

SACRAMENT One of the catechisms defines a sacrament as "the outward and visible sign of an inward and spiritual grace." This points to two aspects of a sacrament: the outward, or seen, action; and the unseen action. A sacrament has its basis in the word and action of Jesus. It is administered by the whole church through recognized members appointed to do this.

Baptism is the sacrament by which the individual becomes a part of the Christian community. It places him within the community of faith where the grace of God strengthens him for the Christian life. Linked with Baptism is confirmation, the laying on of hands. Confirmation is the rite through which a person takes upon himself the promises made for him by parents and/or sponsors at Baptism and receives further strengthening by the Holy Spirit. (See BAPTISM; CONFIRMATION.) In the earliest days of the church, these two actions seem to have occurred on the same occasion. This still happens in the case of adult converts where Baptism and confirmation follow each other closely. In churches that hold to infant Baptism, however, there is a necessary waiting period before the baptized Christian is old enough to know the meaning of the promises made for him. So confirmation follows anywhere from the ages of eight to eighteen. Churches that practice only adult Baptism (Baptists, Disciples) have combined the two rites.

The oldest part of the worship of the church is the Lord's Supper, the meal in which his people, gathered in the presence of God, have remembered God's saving action for them in the death and resurrection of Jesus. Whether the Lord's Supper is held daily, monthly, quarterly, or annually, it has always been a sacred event in which the church members are reminded of their ties to one another in the grace of God given to empower them for daily life in the world. (See LORD'S SUPPER.) Those who repent of their sins and are vitally related to the body of the church partake of this feast. The rite of penance has been the traditional means of preparation for the Holy Communion. (See CONFESSION; PARDON.)

Those who perform the sacred rites need to be chosen and set apart for their function, and ordination symbolizes this action. Marriage, by which the family unit comes into existence, is sanctified by the rite of holy matrimony. Severe illness and the approach to death are signified in the healing and strengthening rite of extreme unction (popularly called by Roman Catholics the "last rites.")

Some Christian groups reject all sacraments (the Society of Friends, for instance), preferring rather to say that there is a sacramental quality to all life. Most Protestant groups recognize two sacraments—Baptism and the Lord's Supper —because these were commanded by Christ himself. Some groups (for instance, the Baptists) refer to these as "ordinances" because they were "ordained" of Christ (see ORDINANCE). The Lutherans have traditionally stressed penance and often have a preparatory service of penance prior to a celebration of the Holy Communion. Catholic communions recognize seven sacraments. Baptism and the Lord's Supper are called the "dominical" sacraments (i.e., from the Lord).

Today the rigidity of numbering these rites is breaking down. It is recognized that in the first centuries of the church the sacramental life was seen with more unity. All the rites indicated outpourings of the grace of God upon his people as they partook of his redemption in Christ. The Easter mysteries (extending from Easter through Pentecost) were marked by services of penance, Baptism-confirmation, the celebration of the Lord's Supper, and ordination. Marriage for many centuries was a civil rite, the religious element being the nuptial Mass.

These rites take the everyday actions of mankind and endow them with sacred significance. Washing becomes the cleansing action of Baptism as the believer dies and rises with Christ. Food and drink become the elements of a sacred meal. The "laying on of hands" symbolizes the gift of the Holy Spirit to strengthen the believer in the Christian life or the person set apart for a special ministry. The joining of hands in marriage suggests the uniting of two lives; the anointing with oil for healing stems from the soothing quality of the oil itself. The inner meaning is reinforced by the outer action. This vivid quality in a sacramental action makes it carry a meaning that words alone could not convey. Sacraments are indeed symbols, and symbols are a language deeper than words.

SACRIFICE A sacrifice is an offering or gift made to God. The purpose is to have communion with God or to make an offering for sin. In the Old Testament a sacrifice might be made in behalf of an individual or of the whole people. There were daily sacrifices and those made on special festival days. The sacrifice was always made at a holy place, such as the Tabernacle or Temple and was offered by a priest in behalf of the people. It should be noted that a sacrifice was never a way of buying forgiveness, for that is a gift of God. It could only express sorrow for sins committed unknowingly. Most sacrifices were of animals, but the meal and wine offerings symbolized other foods used by man. Sometimes the entire offering was burned; sometimes parts became the portion of the priests for their own food.

Usually the sacrifice must be the best of a man's possessions: a perfect lamb or goat, or the first of the grain harvested. This was a recognition that all things came from God and so belonged to him. The firstborn son, however, although equally devoted to God, was always redeemed by the substitution of an animal.

While the sacrifice was given to please God, it was never thought of as a way of buying his favor. It was a return to him of his own. Moreover, the sacrifice was a joyful offering. Today this is lost sight of in popular thought, which speaks of sacrificing as a burden, a giving up.

The sacrificial ceremonies were interrupted by the exile in Babylon, restored when the Temple was rebuilt at Jerusalem about a century later, and finally came to an end with the destruction of that Temple in A.D. 70.

Sometimes the Old Testament writers saw the inadequacies of the sacrificial system. The psalmist knew that a holy life was more acceptable to God than any sacrifice. But the Christians were the first people in the ancient world to abandon the idea of animal sacrifice. They saw in the death of Jesus a pure and perfect sacrifice. He was the lamb substituted for sinful people. He was the ransom through whom his people were freed. His resurrection was the joyful sign of an acceptable sacrifice. One of the meanings of the Lord's Supper is a remembrance of the death of Jesus, an offering of God himself through which man is brought into a new relationship with God.

SAINT Coming from a word that means "holy," the word "saint" means a holy person. "Holy" refers to a person who is set apart as belonging to God. In Christian understanding, it also means a person in whom God's Holy Spirit dwells.

The apostle Paul, in several of his letters, refers to the saints who are "in that place." By this he means that all Christians are saints. This hardly means that they are perfect! They are still human, and he is usually writing to protest some of their ways. It means that at their Baptism, with the laying on of hands, they received the power of the Holy Spirit into their lives. God was with them, helping them to live as Christians. This is why they are saints.

"Saint" is also used in a particular sense. The twelve apostles and Paul are given the title of saint by many branches of the church. During the first few centuries of persecution, the church paid special honor to those who had been killed because of their Christian witness. Martyrs were regarded in a particular sense as saints. A special day has been set aside in the calendar of the church year, November 1, to remember all saints.

Throughout the centuries, more and more people were designated as saints. Finally the church set up standards by which a saint could be recognized as such. Each church was named for a saint. Each person received at confirmation (if not at Baptism) the name of a saint. This was to remind the baptized Christian that he, too, must be a faithful witness.

At the time of the Reformation, Martin Luther felt that the idea of sainthood had been abused. People were celebrating too many saints' days as holidays when these were needed as workdays. The making of a saint seemed to him to have become almost a magical procedure, because of the requirement that a holy person must have performed an acknowledged miracle to become a saint. The New Testament understanding of miracle as a mighty work of God to arouse repentance was being overlooked. Moreover, churches and people collected relics of saints, for the veneration of these was supposed to protect them from harm. Thus the Lutheran and Anglican traditions recognize only the Biblical saints. A day is set apart for each. A church named after a saint will usually have a special celebration on the annual day for remembering that saint (patronal festival).

See HOLINESS.

SALVATION Salvation means "saving." It is related to a word that means "wholeness" and "health." The saved person is one who has been made healthy and whole.

The writers of the Old Testament saw their salvation in terms of God's victory over their enemies. Salvation belonged to God. By his mighty power he had saved them from the armies of Egypt and brought them into the Promised Land.

Salvation in the New Testament is related to the saving from sin and the power of sin (see SIN). Salvation was release from the old life into a new life. This salvation was brought by Jesus Christ. It was a sign that God's power had come among his people in a new way. Illnesses were cured, demons were cast out, and along with these actions, sin was forgiven. When Jesus himself said, "Your sins are for-given" (Mark 2:5), it was an indication that he believed God's saving power resided in himself.

The name Jesus is equivalent to the Hebrew name "Joshua" and means "he who saves." The whole story of the gospel (good news) is that Jesus brought release from the power of sin. He did this because by his every word and action he showed the seeking love of God: walking among people, speaking to them, healing them, warning them of sin and destruction, promising them fullness of life if they turned to God. This utter love and complete obedience reached its climax in the crucifixion. He who was sinless died by the hand of sinful men. But God gave him the victory through the resurrection.

This was the story that the apostles told. Many of those who heard responded to this love. They repented of their sins and knew that God forgave them. They believed in him; they had faith in his power to save. They received from him new life and were enabled by the power of his Holy Spirit to live a different kind of life. They feared neither their own past nor what men could do; they feared neither evil nor death, for they had been saved from all of this.

In order to be saved, a person must know himself to be lost or to be in danger. Those who are satisfied with them-selves feel no need of salvation. God accepts them and transforms them to become worthy of being called by his name. (See JUSTIFICATION.) Salvation is not something to be kept to oneself. It gives an impulse to sharing the good news with others. The life of the church is continued and enriched because it is a fellowship of those who are saved and who are continually bringing others into this same reality.

See REDEMPTION.

SANCTIFICATION   Sanctification means the "process of making holy." In order to understand what that means, one must look at the related word "holy." This is a word that refers to God, to his utter righteousness. "Holy" in the Bible always reflects a quality of being. Other gods might be "holy" because of their power, and the fear that this provoked. The God of Israel was holy because all his acts were righteous, beyond anything that man could attain.

Neither people, places, nor objects can be holy of themselves. They can be made holy only by God. The place of worship is holy because the presence of God fills it; the people of God are holy because he is with them. Holiness is not possessed by any creature; it is granted by God. (See HOLINESS.)

In the New Testament the emphasis is on the sanctification of individuals. This is what God does for those who turn to him through Christ. They are filled with the Holy Spirit. God acts through them, enabling them to live lives that are righteous. This gift is offered through Christ; those who are made holy are the people of God, the church. Sanctification comes at the beginning of the Christian life. It is the power and the process by which Christians are enabled by God to be faithful to him, to serve him by their service to others.

This does not mean that the Christian is one who can live without sin. He is still human. It means that God is with him to help him grow as a Christian. The process is begun by God and continued by him throughout the life of a person. Perfection, however, is never realized in earthly life. (See PERFECTION.)

Sanctification is the process by which God makes his people worthy of being called his sons. There is nothing that a person can do to sanctify himself. All his words and actions, whether toward God or toward people, can only be the expression of what God has done for him. "He disciplines us for our good, that we may share his holiness." (Heb. 12:10.)

See SAINT.

SATAN Satan is the name for an adversary or accuser who brings evildoing to the notice of God, as an adversary would bring wrongdoing to the notice of a king.

Satan is always subordinate to God. He asks God's permission to tempt Job (Job 1:12). In the New Testament he has become the one who is in opposition to God's purposes: he tempts Jesus in the wilderness; he tempts Peter and Judas. He causes disease. He is the leader of the kingdom of evil.

Through his death and resurrection, Christ has overcome the power of Satan, whose works, however, still remain. He tempts the church, but God will have the victory. In the New Testament the devil is identified with Satan. But the words "devils" or "demons" are used for beings under his rule who cause sickness and in other ways inhabit and torment men.

The Biblical understanding about Satan arises from the assurance that human beings can become filled by the Spirit of God. If this be so, it is also possible to be filled by a spirit of evil. This is vividly described by Jesus in a parable where he tells of the possibility that if an unclean spirit were driven out of a person, seven more would quickly enter into the vacancy. (Matt. 12:45.) Only by being filled with the Holy Spirit of God can a person be protected from invasion by demons. The healing of people afflicted by demons was one of the signs that the rule of God had come in Jesus Christ. God alone could overcome evil, and evil could not stand before his presence.

The world is always aware that there seem to be forces of evil stronger than the efforts of individual men toward good. To call the powers of evil "Satan" or "the devil" is to use picture-language in order to describe a force that can be felt but not seen. The writers of the Bible, however, were as certain of the reality of evil in the world as they were certain of the power of God to overcome evil and to cause the triumph of his Kingdom of righteousness.

See EVIL.

SECOND COMING   The understanding of the Second Coming of Christ is bound up with the understanding of judgment.

The Old Testament indicates belief in a day of judgment in which God will punish the peoples of earth for their evil and restore his own people, Israel.

The New Testament writers lived with this belief. It was assumed that the promised One whom God would send on earth would preside at this judgment. The Messiah was called Son of Man and in Christian thought was identified with Jesus, the Christ (Messiah). In both the New Testament and the Creeds of the church there is the affirmation that Christ will come again with glory "to judge the quick and the dead" (The Apostles' Creed).

Jesus had come once to show forth God's love among men and to warn of his judgment. After his resurrection he was seen by many of the disciples, and before he ascended from their sight he promised to send the Holy Spirit among them. They knew him to be among them in their worship, and they knew that his Spirit guided them. Beyond this they expected that a day would come when he would return to earth in the power and glory of God the Father. At first they expected this during their lifetime. Later, they realized that the time was delayed. But they were sure that there would be a specific end to earthly history, at which time the deeds of men would be judged, the evil men thrown into outer darkness and God's faithful servants brought to dwell with him in everlasting light. The Gospels contain several parables of judgment. (Matt. 25:31 ff.; Mark, ch. 13.) The Revelation to John, in highly symbolic language, is assuring a church under persecution that after great violence, Christ will overcome the forces of evil, establish his rule over all the world, and call his people into his city of light.

Some modern writers have thought of the Second Coming in terms of a gradual growth toward perfection in mankind, which would bring about a perfect society. The Biblical writers, however their language is interpreted, had no such idea of development, but saw only a dramatic end to history in the coming of Christ as Judge.

See JUDGMENT.

SERVANT The word "servant" as used in the Bible almost always refers to a slave because at that time all servants were slaves. In the Old Testament this was a limited form of slavery, for the law was careful to outline the conditions under which a person could be held in such bondage. The subjects of a king are also referred to as his servants; likewise, the worshipers of a god are his servants.

In Isaiah there is a series of songs about the servant of God who has been sent to fulfill a special mission in the world. (Isa. 52:13–15; ch. 53.) Through his suffering and death he is exalted by God, and those who recognize that this has been done for them are saved. The New Testament writers see in Jesus the fulfillment of these words, and think of him as this Suffering Servant. (See JESUS CHRIST.)

In the world of the New Testament a slave was often a person who had been born a slave and who could become free only by buying his freedom. His was a life of complete obedience to the will of his master. The New Testament uses this word once of Jesus, when it says that he came in "the form of a servant" (Phil. 2:7). Paul speaks of himself as the slave of Christ, and of Christians as being in bondage to Christ. He used this phrase because by his death Christ had redeemed or bought men from the power of evil (Satan). Now they belonged to him. To Paul this was a bondage to be joyfully accepted and an obedience to be gladly given. He can say that free men are the slaves of Christ and that those who are in human bondage are really free when they belong to Christ because obedience to him makes all other bondage seem lighter. (See I Cor. 7:21–24.)

There is another New Testament word used for "servant" in a specific sense of "giving service to." This word is "minister," meaning "to minister to." This is a voluntary service of helpfulness to another person. The word "deacon" also denotes a "minister" with a special form of service.

Usually when the New Testament speaks of Christians as servants, it means that the servants of God are those who live in complete faithfulness and obedience to him, not questioning his orders, but gladly accepting his demands.

See OBEDIENCE.

SIN Sin is that in man which breaks his relationship to God. Human pride has been called the root of sin, for this is what makes people try to act like God. They attempt to control other people, they are sure that they can "run" their own lives, and they dream of creating a perfect world. (See PRIDE.)

The Bible has several stories to explain sin. (See FALL.) In Gen., ch. 3, there is the story of Adam and Eve in the Garden of Eden. By disobeying God's command, they showed that they did not fully love him or perfectly trust him. The story of the Tower of Babel (Gen., ch. 11) illustrates another aspect of sin. Here were men who were going to build a tower to reach up to heaven (that is, to reach God); this would make them God's equals. But man's pride was overcome in the confusion of languages, and men were scattered over the face of the earth.

The climactic story of the result of man's sin is that of the crucifixion. God came to live among men in the person of Jesus, but man's pride was rebuked by such love. Finally, the leaders of Rome and of Jerusalem crucified him, hoping thus to quiet this unsettling love. The resurrection is God's answer to human sin: an event which indicates that life triumphs over death, love over sin, God over evil.

There are several points to be noticed in an understanding of the word "sin." It is a theological word, that is, it refers to that which happens between God and man. A man can commit a crime against the state; he can do wrong to a neighbor. To the believer in God, such wrongdoing is sin because God has commanded him to love the neighbor. In wronging the neighbor he sins against God. A nonbeliever, however, could speak only of wronging a neighbor.

Another point to notice is that there is a difference between sin (that attitude which separates one from God) and sins (those actions which a person commits). It is not the committing of sins that makes a person sinful, but, rather, the other way around. A person commits sin because he has already separated himself from God. This does not mean

that some people could become so sensitive to the purposes
of God as to become perfectly obedient and always faithful.
Only Jesus was able to do that. It means that those who love
God are aware of his purposes and by his grace are enabled
to fulfill them. Being human, they will sometimes (even
often!) rebel and deliberately choose their own way. Repentance brings forgiveness, and they start anew. (See
OBEDIENCE; REPENTANCE.)

The Bible takes sin seriously. It does not speak of imperfections in people that can be corrected by personal
effort, or mistakes that will be overcome when man knows
what to do. Rather, it says that every person is born with
this desire to act independently of God. Baptized into a
new life in Christ, he is given power to live differently, but
being still human, he often rejects this possibility. It is only
at the end of life that the Christian can say that although
he has sinned, by God's grace he has constantly been brought
back to the source of his life and enabled to live as the child
of God in Christ.

SOUL   In the Bible, man is a whole person comprised of
body and soul. In the Genesis account man is formed, and
God breathes into his nostrils the breath of life: "And man
became a living being" (ch. 2:7). It is difficult to separate
them in Biblical thought, for as the soul indwells the body,
so the body is the covering for the soul. The Bible never
suggests that one is superior to the other: the spiritual and
the material are both part of life.

Although the New Testament often uses the word "spirit"
to refer to the inner self, this can usually be interpreted as
"soul." Sometimes there is the thought of the spirit as the
will, struggling against the body or the flesh, but this is a
struggle within the unity of the person.

Although some ancient peoples believed that the soul
became a disembodied spirit after death, this idea does not
enter into Biblical thinking. Paul speaks of the earthly body's
putting on a spiritual body. (I Cor. 15:44.) The whole per-

son has the gift of eternal life through Christ. When the risen Jesus appeared to his disciples, he had form, so that they recognized him. He was not limited in space and time—he could appear suddenly and disappear before their very eyes —but he had an appearance that was familiar to them. So Christians, taking this as an assurance of their own resurrection from the dead, were sure that God would preserve them as persons and give to each a form for eternal life. This idea is further strengthened by the Biblical understanding of judgment. God asks of each man how he has been faithful, and according to his faithfulness he is rewarded.

In Christian thinking, the soul does not have the limitation of the secular view of "personality," which is dependent upon the body. Neither does it have the limitation of a spiritual view that detaches it from the body. The affirmation of the creeds is belief in the resurrection of the body (The Apostles' Creed) and resurrection of the dead (The Nicene Creed). This is based on the Biblical belief that God is himself personal and that he gives a personal existence to all whom he has created in his own image.

STEWARDSHIP A steward was an important person in Biblical times. Today he would be called a business manager. He was the head employee in the household of a king, a member of the nobility or some wealthy person. It was his responsibility to hire and fire other employees, to pay them wages and see that they did their work properly. He kept accounts and presented them to his employer; he even invested money and was responsible for its increase. He was a valuable and a trusted servant. He might even be a slave, owned by and completely in the power of his master.

The Bible assumes that all people are stewards for God. The parable of the unforgiving steward is a reminder of this relationship. (Matt. 18:23–35.) The master forgave the steward his debts, but the steward then went among his creditors forcing them to pay what they owed him. The result was that the master punished the steward. Another steward, who, when asked for an accounting, sought but a partial payment from his master's creditors, was commended for his wisdom. (Luke 16:1–16.) Forgiveness is a quality of the steward who recognizes this relationship to his Master, on whom he depends for forgiveness. The steward has a responsibility (Luke 12:42 f.) and he must be ready at any time to greet the return of his Master and give an account of how he has carried out his Master's commands. For, as the apostle Paul wrote to the church at Corinth, "It is required of stewards that they be found trustworthy [that is, faithful]" (I Cor. 4:2).

The picture of the steward, then, is used in the New Testament as a description of every person. God is the Creator; all things and people belong to him. Man did not create himself, nor does he own the world. He was placed in the world and given dominion over the earth by God, his loving Creator. For this reason, everything that he "owns," he holds as a trust from God. It is not his to do with as he pleases. Even his own life is not his own; this, too, belongs to God. Someday the Lord will ask each person, "What did you do with the life I have given you?" and "What did you do in the world over which I gave you power?" The answer will indicate the extent to which the person recognized that neither life nor the world was a personal possession.

The New Testament parables about stewards and the references to stewardship indicate several qualities of the good steward. He listens carefully to his Lord's commands and carries them out obediently. He is faithful to his Lord, being sensitive to his requirements and putting his work above all personal interests. He is merciful to others, forgiving them when they abuse him, asking less of them than he asks of himself.

The Old Testament speaks of the "tithe," a plan whereby every faithful member of the people of Israel sets aside one tenth of his possessions (and earnings) for the service of God. These were the offerings made at the Temple. The New Testament never speaks of the tithe. It does not mention the amount—either in time or in money—that is owed to God. It is assumed that everything is owed to him and that he expects complete surrender and obedience of the self, because love does not know halfway measures. "God so loved the world that he gave his only Son." (John 3:16.) This is told again and again in the Christian church and is the basis for the Christian insistence that men cannot love God less than he loves them.

See OFFERING.

SYMBOL A symbol is a word picture. The actual picture itself (sign, symbol) never changes its form, but the meaning of a symbol may become enlarged, deepened, and even acquire varying emphases, although its essential meaning remains the same. Symbols are used in place of words. People who cannot read words can understand the same symbol.

The cross is the central symbol of the Christian faith. As a simple picture, it is nothing more than an ancient instrument used for death by torture. To the Christian, however, that meaning is far in the background. The important thing for him is the purpose of Christ's death on the cross. Its meaning lies in what it tells about God's love. It is a reminder of what sinful human beings can do when they determine to thwart God. It has helped many people to endure suffering bravely as true followers of Jesus.

A symbol may take the form of a picture, an object, or alphabetical letters. There is the alpha and omega symbol: the Greek letters at the beginning and at the end of the alphabet; they remind one that God is the beginning and end of all things. There are symbols to suggest an understanding of God as Trinity: a triangle, a trefoil, or three intertwined rings. Each of the twelve apostles has been given a symbol suggestive of his work. The chalice is a symbol of the Lord's Supper. The vine is a reminder that the Christian lives only as his life is sustained by Christ: "I am the vine, you are the branches" (John 15:5).

The interior of a church usually contains symbols. When

a person sits in church, waiting for the service to begin, he can look at each symbol and see what it tells him about God and where it reminds him of the words of the Bible. Such symbols are used in two ways: they prepare a person for worship, and they teach him something about the Christian faith.

A symbol need not be a visual image; it can be spoken words. The Apostles' Creed has been called the Roman Symbol because it was first used among Christians in Rome as their confession of faith. This brief statement has meaning beyond the bare words and so is rightly called a symbol (as is any creed). A religious rite contains symbolic actions: the pouring of water in baptism, the use of the ring in the marriage service. The action suggests deeper meaning.

Symbols make it possible for Christian people to understand their faith, although they may differ in language, nationality, and even in time.

T

TEMPTATION   "The temptation" is the period when Jesus, after his baptism by John the Baptist, went into the wilderness region. There he spent forty days alone. He must have prayed, thought, and wrestled with the meaning of the ministry to which he now knew God had called him. He also faced the question as to the means he would use for his work for God. (See Mark 1:12–13; Matt. 4:1–11; Luke 4:1–13.) During this period there occurred the experience in which, the Gospels report, he was "tempted by Satan" (see SATAN).

Jesus' temptation took the form of symbolic choices. Turning stones into bread may refer to a temptation to use material means in the promotion of God's Kingdom—appealing to comfort, promising things. Or it could mean that he was tempted to seek his own welfare at the same time he proclaimed the gospel. Leaping from the top of the Temple was a temptation to use spectacular methods for calling attention to his message and plan. The temptation to win the kingdoms of the world suggests the use of political rather than spiritual power. In each case Jesus responds by rejecting the temptation, using deep insights that had come to him from the Jewish Scriptures.

By firmly refusing to yield to these tempting suggestions from Satan, Jesus gained strength for the difficult task to which God had called him. Later, reflecting on Jesus, the author of Hebrews wrote that he was "one who in every respect has been tempted as we are, yet without sinning" (ch. 4:15).

Everyone is faced with temptation. In many situations of life, one has to make decisions and choices. Oftentimes these decisions and choices involve the possibility of doing something that would be advantageous and pleasing in personal terms but would hurt another and damage one's own character in the long run. The evil choice to which one is tempted is often difficult to resist because it is appealing and exciting.

The Lord's Prayer contains the petition, "Lead us not into temptation, but deliver us from evil." In teaching his followers to pray thus, Jesus spoke out of his own experience, for he, too, had been tempted. Also, he was familiar with the prayers spoken every morning and evening by each devout Jew, containing the petition, "Bring us not into the hand of any temptation." This does not mean that God is asked to keep people from being tempted. Life is bound to bring temptation. Rather, it means that God is asked to help in temptation that they may be strong enough to resist the evil choice. In this sense the prayer means, "Lead us not into situations in which, when we are tested, we shall not be able to do the right thing." God does not lead people into temptation in order to encourage them to sin. Instead, he helps the tempted person by giving him strength to face temptation and to resist it.

TEN COMMANDMENTS   There are two listings of the Ten Commandments in the Old Testament. The oldest listing is in Ex. 20:1–17. The book of Deuteronomy, written as a retelling of the law, contains this material in ch. 5:6–21. For the Hebrews this set of Ten Commandments was considered basic to the covenant between God and man. Other laws would have to be made for the people from time to time to cover changing situations and needs. But these had the character of basic laws given directly by God himself, on which all other rules and regulations must be based. The Ten Commandments are sometimes called the Decalogue, meaning " ten words."

The Shema, repeated frequently by devout Jews, was a reminder to the people of this fundamental law of the covenant: "Hear, O Israel: The Lord our God is one Lord; and you shall love the Lord your God with all your heart, and with all your soul, and with all your might" (Deut. 6:4–5). The people are commanded to write these laws in their hearts, and to be ever mindful of them while walking, when lying down to sleep, and when rising. God, who has given his commandment, will also be faithful to his promises. He gives his law because of his promise to be with his people and to lead them into the Promised Land.

The Ten Commandments were inherited by Christians from Judaism. Jesus, too, assumed that these commandments were binding on all. However, he put an emphasis on keeping the law because the law is given by God to show us his own love that is always back of the law. To a question as to what is the greatest commandment, Jesus replied in the word of the Shema. He continued with a quotation from Leviticus, "The second is this, 'You shall love your neighbor as yourself' " (Mark 12:31, quoting Lev. 19:18). This is often referred to as Jesus' "summary of the law." It is frequently used in Christian worship services: "On these two commandments depend all the law and the prophets" (Matt. 22:40).

Those who truly love God will not keep the commandments merely because they are law. They love the neighbor because this is the heart of the relationship between God and man. Christians are called to obey a God of love. They are first of all to live "in the Spirit." The life thus lived will show the "fruit of the Spirit," which Paul describes as "love, joy, peace, patience, kindness, goodness, faithfulness, gentleness, self-control" (Gal. 5:22–23).

TIME Each year when a person's birthday turns up on the calendar he thinks more about the passage of time than on any other date. New Year is also a reminder of this. He must start writing the new year on letters, and he finds that for a few days after January 1 he is still putting down last year's number.

Actually, time is an idea that can be grasped only in terms of measurement. It is said that a certain person was born in a particular year and lived for eighty years. That gives a measurable amount of time. Historians talk of centuries: Columbus discovered San Salvador in 1492, or air transport developed in the first half of the twentieth century. This is called chronological time, that is, time that can be measured in terms of specific dates and periods.

There is another way to think of time: periods in which certain events happen that are of greatest significance for the world. This is not something that can be measured, for the meaning of a period can be understood only by looking back at the events involved. The Jewish-Christian religious tradition speaks of this kind of time when it points to the events recorded in the Bible. In some cases these events are impossible to date exactly. They were events in which the Biblical writers were sure they could see God's hand at work doing something of greatest importance for the human race.

All time is in God's charge. Some periods of time seemed especially prepared by God for certain events to take place. Such was the exodus of Israel from Egypt. Such was the culmination of the Jewish hope for a Messiah (Savior) in the coming of Jesus. Looking back on these events, the Biblical writers saw them as times when God entered actively into history. He is always in control of history, and the end of time as well as its beginning and its continuance are his responsibility, not man's. But these special times were so important as to change the life of mankind forever afterward. The importance of Jesus for the world's salvation was emphasized when the very calendar itself, measuring time, was changed to the years Before Christ and to *Anno Domini* (in the year of the Lord).

Time is not just a blank for the Christian. He knows that time is the setting into which he has been placed by God in the world. His task is to use the time given on earth in such a way as to seek to fulfill God's purposes for him and for the age. This is true both of the individual's life-span and of the total life of the race in a particular time. "Look carefully then how you walk, not as unwise men but as wise, making the most of the time, because the days are evil. Therefore do not be foolish, but understand what the will of the Lord is." (Eph. 5:15–17.)

TRINITY   The word "Trinity" will not be found in the New Testament, but it has been one of the most important words in the vocabulary of the Christian church.

When the parts of the word are examined, they really mean tri-unity, "three in one." The theologians of the early church sought to explain the relationship of God the Father to Jesus, the Son of God, and to the Holy Spirit. Many different ideas were advanced as to how the Father, Son, and Holy Spirit were connected. Finally, at church councils in Nicaea (A.D. 325) and Constantinople (A.D. 381) the leaders of the church stated that God, Jesus Christ, and the Holy Spirit are of the same being with one another. That is, God is not divided in his nature. But he is known to us as the Heavenly Father who created and sustains the world and all that is; as the Son, who redeems mankind; and as the Holy Spirit, who is the continuing presence of God in the world through the risen Christ.

Sometimes people are confused by the doctrine of the Trinity. They think this means that there are three separate "Persons." This is not what the Trinity means. There is only one God, who makes himself known to us through the Son and through the Holy Spirit.

Although the New Testament does not use the word "Trinity," it became important because the New Testament writers had already referred to the relationship of Father, Son, and Holy Spirit that later were developed into the doctrine of the Trinity. Paul closes a letter with these words, often used as a benediction in church services: "The grace of the Lord Jesus Christ and the love of God and the fellowship of the Holy Spirit be with you all" (II Cor. 13:14).

Matthew's Gospel closes with words attributed to the risen Christ: "Go therefore and make disciples of all nations, baptizing them in the name of the Father and of the Son and of the Holy Spirit, teaching them to observe all that I have commanded you; and lo, I am with you always, to the close of the age" (ch. 28:19–20). Since the Gospel uses a trinitarian form, if not the word "Trinity," in attributing these words to the Lord himself, it may perhaps be assumed that the Trinity way of thinking must have been in the mind of the church from the earliest times.

TRUTH Philosophers from early Greek times on have asked the question, What is true? Some have thought they were able to give final answers to that question. Others have pointed out the difficulties in trying to state the truth, and have said that there is no such thing as something that is true for all men everywhere. Some have thought that truth is like beauty and goodness—ideals seldom achieved in human experience but standards toward which men ought to strive. Others have said that nothing is true except what works in actual situations.

In Christian faith, however, the word is used in another sense. The Bible does not think of "truth" as something abstract that the mind of man can figure out. It teaches that only what comes from God is true. If the heart is open to God's love, one will be able to live according to his truth. As Ps. 51:6 puts it: "Behold, thou desirest truth in the inward being; therefore teach me wisdom in my secret heart."

Christians regard truth as a way of life that involves their relationship to Jesus Christ. Instead of looking for truth in the abstract, they look at Jesus. In his life, ministry, and teachings they see truth in action. Jesus himself is cited as saying: "If you continue in my word, you are truly my disciples, and you will know the truth, and the truth will make you free." (John 8:31–32.) Again he says, "I am the way, and the truth, and the life; no one comes to the Father, but by me." (John 14:6.) The Christian believes that truth will be found as he needs it in particular situations if he faithfully follows Christ.

Truth does involve the use of the mind to find correct information. A person should be able to tell the difference between actual facts and mere rumors. The writer of The Third Letter of John had caught, however, the deeper meaning of truth as Jesus revealed it—a way of life—when he wrote to a church member named Gaius: "For I greatly rejoiced when some of the brethren arrived and testified to the truth of your life, as indeed you do follow the truth. No greater joy can I have than this, to hear that my children follow the truth" (vs. 3–4).

V

VOCATION The word "vocation" refers to being "called" or "summoned." The word is sometimes used to refer to choosing work in a particular vocation or field, such as business, law, nursing, or farming. But in Christian theology "vocation" has the meaning of "God's call" to a life that is answered by loyal, faithful service. The Christian is called to be a member of the church. He is also called to think through the whole of life's meaning in the light of what can best be understood to be his purpose. One then seeks to fulfill this purpose by walking with him through all of life, trusting in his guidance. The word "vocation" comes from a Latin word meaning "to call."

Sometimes the word is used in another sense, referring to "Christian vocations." In this case the meaning is nearer to what was referred to above as working in particular fields. In the church, too, there is work to be done by those who feel that God has called them to full-time occupations in religion as ministers, missionaries, directors of Christian education, workers with youth, writers, editors of religious publications, teachers of religion in schools, colleges, seminaries, and so on. Those who decide to serve God through the church in these ways are required to go through special schooling in order to prepare themselves for usefulness in such work.

Every Christian is called to serve God through his particular field of work. It is just as important to have Christian physicians, business people, politicians, and policemen (or Christians in any field of work) as it is to have persons devoting all their time specifically to church work.

W

WISDOM "Wise" persons are usually thought of as those who have a fine education and whose minds are trained to think clearly. Of course, not all educated people can be called "wise." Usually that term is reserved for those who seem to stand out above others as having special insight and understanding. Think of schoolteachers. Some seem "wiser" than others. It is not always easy to decide just what makes them so. Usually they not only know a great deal about their subjects but are able to relate what they know to the whole meaning of life.

In the ancient world the Greeks thought of philosophers and writers of tragedies as wise persons. The Hebrews were more interested in practical wisdom. Those were considered wise who could apply knowledge to the actual situations in which people found themselves living. Some gained a reputation for being wise because they were able to state things in memorable ways, for example, the writers of The Proverbs, Job, or Ecclesiastes.

The Hebrews thought true wisdom was not possible unless it was related to God. God is the source of wisdom. The wise person is the one who listens to the commandments of God and lives his life in accordance with them. The psalmist writes: "The fear of the Lord is the beginning of wisdom; a good understanding have all those who practice it." (Ps. 111:10.) In Job the question is asked: "Where shall wisdom be found? And where is the place of understanding?" (ch. 28:12). God answers man, "Behold, the fear of the Lord, that is wisdom; and to depart from evil is understanding." (V. 28.) Wisdom is God's gift to those who seek understanding from his hand.

King Solomon gained the reputation in the tradition of Israel as having been a very wise man. Jesus is not portrayed in the Gospels as primarily wise, although some who heard him in his hometown synagogue could not understand how one they had known as a local carpenter's son could have so much profound knowledge. "Where did this man get all this? What is the wisdom given to him?" (Mark 6:2.) Jesus' wisdom was due to God's life in him. Later, Paul said that Jesus possessed true wisdom because "in him all the fulness of God was pleased to dwell" (Col. 1:19). Jesus Christ *is* wisdom, for "he is before all things, and in him all things hold together" (Col. 1:17).

It is possible for a person to be wise in the sense of having deep understanding about many things. Such wisdom does not necessarily require religious foundations. The religious person will have deep understanding about the most important thing in life—God's will for him. This is spiritual wisdom, the greatest gift of all, a gift from God rather than the result of man's own ability to think.

WITNESS   The English word "witness" means the same as the Greek word *martyr* does. A witness is one who testifies to what is true for him even by giving up his life. The martyrs of the church have always been its most effective witnesses. They include those Christians who were devoured by wild beasts in the Coliseum during the persecutions by Rome. They also include missionaries of the present time who have lost their lives by seeking to take the gospel to primitive tribesmen in remote places.

However, a witness is not only someone who loses his life because of his faith. The word "witness" includes anyone who confesses before men by word and deed what the Christian gospel is and what it means to him. For some this will mean speaking about the Christian faith to others, personally or before audiences. Preachers are witnesses in this sense. So are laymen who explain their faith to others and find opportunities through conversation and deeds of loving-kindness to express the meaning of their faith in action.

The whole church also witnesses through its corporate life. When Christians gather to worship God in word and sacrament, they witness to one another for the strengthening of their common faith. When the church is true to its real nature it always seeks to bring others into the worshiping community. Furthermore, it goes into the world and ministers in the name and Spirit of Christ to all who have needs of any kind. Sometimes the church's concern for the suffering (shown through providing hospitals, schools, and extending fellowship to the lonely) is a more powerful witness to the world than all the words spoken about religion.

See MARTYR.

WORD OF GOD In the ancient world the word spoken by a person was thought to be an extension of the person himself. For example, when a blessing was pronounced (such as that of Isaac on Jacob), it had a lasting effect that could not be wiped out. If a king gave an order to one of his subjects, it was an order that had to be obeyed. The word spoken was bound up with the speaker's purpose. Thus when people considered how God's will was to be known it was assumed to be by the word he himself spoke. Since God was invisible and could not be heard to speak actual words, his word was considered to come to them through the lips of holy men, prophets, seers, and persons especially selected by him to be the carriers of his word to the people. Thus Moses delivered the covenant that God made with the people of Israel.

The word of God was not like any other word, however. Because there was only one God, his word had a power and an authority above all other words. Thus the word of God was thought of as a command. Because God had spoken it, it could not be ignored. Because he was faithful to his promises, it would be fulfilled. Thus it is written in Isa. 55:11, "So shall my word be that goes forth from my mouth; it shall not return to me empty, but it shall accomplish that which I purpose, and prosper in the thing for which I sent it." This understanding of the faithfulness and power of God was different from that of certain other religions, which thought that by magic rites or ceremonies it would be possible to cause a god to do what the people wanted him to do.

The word of God is the manner in which communication between God and man takes place. If God did not communicate with his people, they would not know who and what he is and what he expects of them. Jesus spoke so clearly in word and deed about God that his followers knew him to be the Son of God. Now people could know the fullness of life with God because the word of God had been spoken by a man who walked on earth as other men did, but with the difference that there was no barrier between himself and God. Hence when the writer of the Fourth Gospel started his book, he said of Jesus: "The Word became flesh and dwelt among us" (John 1:14). (See INCARNATION.)

Because the Bible contains the record of God's word given to man through Israel and through Jesus Christ and the apostles, the whole Bible itself is sometimes referred to as the Word of God. This understanding is made clear in the words sometimes used to introduce the reading of the Bible in church services: "Hear the Word of God as it is contained in the book of . . ." The Bible is not the Word of God in the sense that every word in it was divinely "dictated." Rather, in these writings men have recorded the word of God as channeled through the history and experiences that they preserved.

WORSHIP Worship is characteristic of people in all times and places. It is the giving of respectful devotion to what is regarded as the most powerful and highest reality in the world. In a very broad sense it might be possible to say that where material things are regarded as of supreme value, man worships those *things;* possessions, nation, power, for example.

Normally worship refers to the veneration of the divine. The various world religions interpret the divine in different ways. In Buddhism and Hinduism, since the divine is considered to be a completely otherwordly force or principle, the worshipers direct their thoughts toward escape from this world and its entanglements. The Jewish-Christian religion, however, emphasizes God as personal—that is, as One who can be known only because he reveals himself.

Worship includes both individuals' coming into God's presence in prayer and the corporate action of an entire congregation. Individual prayer and meditation are more properly to be thought of as devotions. Worship occurs when there is a blending of many persons in a joint offering of prayer and praise to God. The expression "service of worship" is used because worship is a joint action of serving God. Worship is spoken of as "offered" to God by the people.

Worship is a two-way process. It includes the offering (service) to God. But it means also that he is meeting his people. Jesus said, "Where two or three are gathered in my name, there am I in the midst of them." (Matt. 18:20.) The Holy Spirit meets those gathered in Christ's name. He is an active presence in the worship of the church. This means that worship is much more than getting together to sing hymns, say prayers, and listen to a sermon. It means that through the liturgy (literally, the "work of the people") the congregation is reminded of the active presence of God in their midst. By word and sacrament they are strengthened to be faithful to God's call to serve him both in the church and in the world.

See CEREMONY; LITURGY; RITUAL.

WRATH In ancient Greek and Roman religions, it was thought that the gods had "moods." Sometimes they got very angry with people. Zeus (Jupiter) would hurl his thunderbolts through the sky in order to show anger. In many primitive religions various sacrifices, even sometimes of human beings, were offered to the gods in order to try to please them. If the gods grew angry, they might not permit the crops to grow into a good harvest, and the people would starve.

Biblical religion thinks of God quite differently from this. It has been said that God detests sin but always loves the sinner. God never hates persons but he shows his displeasure against the sin that keeps them away from him. His wrath is his hatred for sin. He is forever wanting the sinner to receive his mercy and his love.

Sometimes people get so wrapped up in selfishness that they forget God. Everything seems to go along very well without him, so they seldom if ever bother to pray to him, to thank him, or to worship him. If they wake up some day to realize that they really are not self-sufficient after all, but need God's help more than they had ever imagined, they realize how real God's wrath is. Only a person who knows God's love can also know that God judges men and hates their sins.